Engaging Others, Knowing Ourselves

A Lutheran Calling in a Multi-Religious World

Carol Schersten LaHurd, Editor

Darrell Jodock and Kathryn Mary Lohre,
Consulting Editors

Lutheran University Press
Minneapolis, Minnesota

Engaging Others, Knowing Ourselves:
A Lutheran Calling in a Multi-Religious World

Carol Schersten LaHurd, Editor

Darrell Jodock and Kathryn Mary Lohre, Consulting Editors

Copyright © 2016 Evangelical Lutheran Church in America

Prepared by the ELCA Consultative Panels on Lutheran-Jewish and Lutheran-Muslim Relations and the Office of the Presiding Bishop, Ecumenical and Inter-Religious Relations

Cover photograph by Sarah Bromberger, Augustana College (Rock Island) class of 2016, of participants at the first Interfaith Understanding Conference, June 1-3, 2014. The mural, entitled "Cadence of Diversity," was painted by more than fifty Augustana students in 2009-2010, led by art professor Peter Xiao.

ISBN: 978-1-942304-13-5

Lutheran University Press, PO Box 390759, Minneapolis, MN 55439
www.lutheranupress.org
Printed in the United States of America

Table of Contents

Foreword

Elizabeth A. Eaton, presiding bishop

In August 2014, just one year after my election as presiding bishop of the Evangelical Lutheran Church in America (ELCA), I flew into Detroit on the Friday of Labor Day weekend. I had been invited by our longtime partner and friend, Dr. Sayyid Syeed, national director for the Office of Interfaith and Community Alliances, to bring greetings to the 30,000 American Muslims gathering for the annual convention of the Islamic Society of North America (ISNA).

Dr. Syeed was the first Muslim speaker to greet our Churchwide Assembly in 2011, on the tenth anniversary of 9/11. He had described how "during the last millennium mountains of hate [and] discrimination have been built. Our job," he said, "is to see those mountains of hate removed." He reminded us that "no particular church, no particular religious community, no nation on earth can fight those mountains of misunderstanding alone. It is a collective responsibility, and we have already started our work in that direction." He was received by the assembly with a standing ovation.

Nevertheless, on the taxi ride from the airport to the convention center in Detroit, I became aware that my presence with ISNA was causing a stir among some members of the ELCA. Calls and emails had been pouring into the churchwide offices that morning, asking for an explanation of why I was, as one prominent headline falsely suggested, "keynoting a fundraiser for Hamas." I was saddened and discouraged by the ostensible gulf between these two experiences.

Over the next several days, we sought to respond to each inquiry. We lifted up the ELCA's commitments to inter-religious relations, dating back to the Constituting Convention in 1987. We shared the history of our Muslim relations, as a counter-cultural witness for peace in the years following 9/11. We gave examples of how we had partnered with ISNA on issues of common concern, including religious freedom, poverty, gun violence, and the Middle East. We defended against the notion that Islam is a religion of violence or that ISNA is a terrorist organization. But perhaps, most importantly, we spoke of our calling as Lutherans in a multi-religious society to love our neighbors—of all religious traditions, and none—and to defend and speak well of them, as Luther reminds us in his explanation of the eighth commandment.

Admittedly, our responses were not always met with satisfaction. What this all made crystal clear to me is that we as a church are in dire need of a dialogue of praxis about what it means to be Lutheran Christians in a multi-religious society. We all live and work in an increasingly multi-ethnic, inter-religious context. In our daily encounter with diversity, what are the theological and practical challenges we face? What from our Lutheran tradition is instructive for understanding our inter-religious calling and living out our commitments? How might we work together, in the practice of communal discernment, to seek God's vision for the inter-religious life of the ELCA?

This book invites us all into such a conversation by challenging us to reflect on our past, learn from our present, and envision the future to which God is calling us. The heart of the book is the real-life case studies of inter-religious relations unfolding in a variety of ELCA ministry contexts. They encourage us to understand that our questions, doubts, and failures are as important as our answers, convictions, and successes. They challenge us to embrace the fact that while there are a variety of responses to religious plurality, our common response is rooted in our Lutheran vocation—our response to God's love in Jesus Christ.

It is no coincidence that the authors of this project are those long-time scholars, pastors, and practitioners whom I have appointed to advise me on matters of Lutheran-Jewish and Lutheran-Muslim relations, to create educational resources for the inter-religious life of this church, and to care for this church's relations with several of our closest bi-lateral and multi-lateral partners. Their expertise is of the highest quality, and this book is their gift to the church at this critical time. I am deeply grateful for their remarkable work to shepherd this project from an idea into a reality. A special thank you to all those across this church who have contributed their stories to this enterprise and to Lutheran University Press for supporting the vision of this project.

ELCA Lutheran-Jewish and Lutheran-Muslim Panel members, who began planning for this book in October 2012 (l to r): Esther Menn, Jonathan Brockopp, Mark Swanson, Carol Schersten LaHurd, Skip Cornett, Darrell Jodock, Peg Schultz-Akerson, Paul Rajashekar, Peter M. Makari, Kathryn Lohre. Not pictured: Peter Pettit, Nelly Van Doorn Harder.

We know that we are freed in Christ to love and serve our neighbors. But in a time of rapid change, we might spend a moment considering the age-old question, "And who is my neighbor?" Today our neighbors represent the spectrum of the world's religions, the diversity of global Christianity, and the rising tide of secularization. This reality demands something new of us. Let's start by asking the good Lutheran question "What does this mean?" and then move from there, better equipped to live out our vocation as Lutherans in a multi-religious world.

A Pastor and a Professor on
Why This Book?

Esther Menn and Peg Schultz-Akerson

The bold purpose of this book is not dialogue between religions but discovery of the religiously-other neighbor as a fellow pilgrim whose questions and ponderings matter for our life together. The world is small, and one good way to fulfill our vocational call to serve and honor our neighbors is to come to know them in deepened relationships across our various communities of belonging. This vocational call to service wisely includes learning also what it means to be recipients of service from the neighbor. Real community happens within such giving and receiving because it calls us not only to be the trusted ones but also to humbly entrust our needs to the neighbor.

Rightfully, this book assumes you, the reader, have your own stories and that your participation as dialogue partner will add to the nearly fifty stories others yearned to share because their inter-religious encounters profoundly shaped their lives. Organized in four groupings, a wide range of case studies provide stimulus for deepened reflection and further engagement. To this end, the book's sending words assert, "Its next chapter is in your hands."

As a parish pastor, I (Peg Schultz-Akerson) have had the joy of serving a congregation that shared a worship space and, more delicately, a kitchen with a kosher-observing synagogue. I've known the intensity of being called upon to support a grieving Muslim family facing an unexpected emergency room death. I have not yet participated in meditation practices with Buddhists in a prison setting or walked with a congregant whose study of Hinduism led to unexpected conversation about what it means to live faithfully as a Christian. Some of the vignettes here may resonate with your own experiences, but the array is so rich that it is sure to provide many you may not yet have imagined.

Rather than gloss over challenges involved in deepened inter-religious connection, these chapters support us to engage them with honoring ears, thirsty curiosity, and informed theological and historical background. There are paradoxes, for instance, regarding differing views of God toward which this resource is not an "answer" book but an encouragement to grow relationships of trust as goal and gift.

How good it is to be challenged by our own faith community to recognize how engrained, historic, and harmful our own religious stereotypes remain and to be given tools and suggestions fashioned by Lutheran theological and scriptural insight to support a dismantling of them. There is hard work here to be sure, but work coupled with ample support for honoring a Christian understanding of the vocational call to transformative engagement with God's diverse world. This hard work is beloved work because engaging relationally with religious communities beyond our own poises us for participation where God is afoot in our daily reality of religious pluralism.

As a seminary professor and dean, I (Esther Menn) have found the case studies approach especially promising for theological education today. Those preparing to be pastors and lay leaders will be encouraged and inspired by learning about what others are doing in congregational and community settings through concrete examples. Each of the full-text case studies interspersed throughout the chapters emphasizes the importance of building relationships with people from different religions traditions. These inter-religious friendships open us to new and often unexpected insights and directions in worship, theological reflection, and social action.

The action-reflection model, starting from the grass-roots level of lived experience and then reflecting on that experience in theological terms, is one that can be used productively, starting in seminaries, colleges, and universities, and continuing in churches and communities.

Another strength of the book is the inclusion of interdisciplinary approaches to inter-religious relations, including practical, theological, historical, and ethical dimensions. These various lenses highlight the richness and blessing of our life together in these changing times, when our churches, families, and communities are facing change and opportunity for cooperation and reconciliation.

The book also provides a wealth of resources for further study. Far from attempting a comprehensive and conclusive treatment, this book offers an access point for further inter-religious engagement at the ground level. The information boxes embedded in each chapter highlight key concepts and flag additional content helpful for the classroom and other learning contexts. Questions placed at the end of each chapter serve as catalysts for further discussion and ongoing grappling with central issues. The bibliography included in the footnotes and the helpful websites listed in the appendix chart possible next steps in learning about and engaging our inter-religious neighbors. For additional ideas, the study guide in the appendix, "Ways to Use This Book," points the way forward.

The many resources included in this book are intended to support the imagination and the initiative of those in the ELCA and in other Christian denominations to reach out to our neighbors for friendship, practical assistance, theological learning, and social action for the common good.

> Far from attempting a comprehensive and conclusive treatment, the book offers an access point for further inter-religious engagement at the ground level.

May our encounters here awaken fresh curiosity, not only to learn of other religious practices but, most importantly, to come to know people who practice religion differently than we. May we discover that they, like we, are beautifully and marvelously made in God's good image and desire to engage God's vision of a healed and whole creation. "O taste and see that the LORD is good" (Psalm 34:8, NRSV).

INTRODUCTION

Time-Tested Questions

Darrell Jodock

The subtitle of this book identifies inter-religious conversation and cooperation as "A Lutheran Calling in a Multi-Religious World." Why the word "Lutheran"? It is there not to suggest that this "calling" or this book is intended only for Lutherans. Nor does it claim that Lutherans have some totally unique perspective on inter-religious relations. While the book occasionally appeals to themes more emphasized by Luther and his followers than by other Christians, these themes are not missing from other Christian traditions and thus are profitably explored by all. The word "Lutheran" in the subtitle serves to acknowledge as candidly as possible the theological perspective of the book's authors. It also suggests to those readers who may themselves be Lutheran that its recommendations have roots in their own tradition. And the word acknowledges that the perspective throughout is Christian. What this book reflects is not an outsider's view but the perspective of persons within the Christian community who have experienced inter-religious dialogue and cooperation. The editors and authors expect the book to be useful for an audience much wider than the Lutheran community. In other words, though written *by* Lutherans, the book is not intended only *for* Lutherans.

The subtitle also anticipates the 500th anniversary of the Reformation, to be observed October 31, 2017. Luther's 95 Theses were written in the context of Christendom—a society, that is, which granted a privileged position to the church and its priorities. Citizenship was open only to Christians. And only orthodox Christian teachings were allowed in public. Sometimes Jews and Muslims were tolerated, sometimes not. But in Western Europe four centuries would pass before non-Christians would be allowed to become citizens. Today's context is different. The United States has no "established" religion. There is no religious test for citizenship. Religious diversity is evident in our schools, our places of work, and our neighborhoods, and every religion has equal status before the law. Given this change from Christendom to religious pluralism, what does the Reformation heritage mean today? How are Christians to treat their religiously diverse neighbors? This book intends to make a modest contribution to this discussion by claiming that in our day the legacy of the Reformation includes a calling to engage with our neighbors and to seek inter-religious understanding and cooperation. In the subtitle, the word "Lutheran" signals this book's concern with the contemporary implications of the Reformation tradition. Within ecumenical Christianity, it is a concern not reserved for Lutherans alone. How the Reformation is understood in one way or another affects every branch of Christianity, to say nothing about the wellbeing of society as a whole.

One of the greatest challenges for churches today is to navigate the intersection between ecumenical and inter-religious relations. What it means to be a Christian in a multi-religious world must be explored both via exchanges with ecumenical partners and via a re-examination of the resources of one's own denominational tradition. The benefits go both ways. The results from ecumenical conversations about this topic can inform the interpretation of one's own denominational tradition, and explorations of that one tradition can inform ecumenical understanding and practice. While mindful of the importance of ecumenical explorations of inter-religious relations and drawing on those explorations, this book arises out of experiences and discussions within one denomination—namely, the Evangelical Lutheran Church in America. What gifts does it have to offer its own members and its ecumenical partners as they ponder the question of being Christian in a multi-religious world?

How did a book of this sort come to be? This question can be answered in two ways. First, from a longer-term perspective, by tracing some developments in the ELCA that have led to this point in inter-religious relations. Second, by describing a process, starting in 2012, that led more specifically to this book. This introduction will examine both, considering each in turn.

Background Developments

Two consultative panels currently work with and advise the ELCA Office of the Presiding Bishop, one focusing on Lutheran-Jewish relations and the other on Lutheran-Muslim relations. The first was formed in 1989, only a year after the ELCA came together. It was able to build on

Lutheran-Jewish consultations which had been going on since the 1960s. The second panel was organized in 2008, in part in response to 9/11. Both have been available to provide advice to the presiding bishop and other church leaders regarding Jewish-Lutheran or Muslim-Lutheran relations. Both have produced educational materials for use in the church. And each has maintained contacts with leaders in the Jewish and the Muslim communities. In recent years the panels have stayed in touch with each other, held joint meetings, and sought ways to cooperate.

Let us consider first the work of the Consultative Panel on Lutheran-Jewish Relations. Its initial task was to help draft the "Declaration of the Evangelical Lutheran Church in America to the Jewish Community," which was adopted by the ELCA Church Council in April 1994. This declaration rejected Luther's harsh recommendations regarding the Jews made in 1543 (urging that synagogues be closed, Jewish books be confiscated, safe travel be rescinded, and so on). It pledged the Church to work against anti-Semitism and resolved that the ELCA live out its faith "with love and respect for the Jewish people."[1] Addressed to the Jewish community, it was received there with much appreciation. For example, the U.S. Holocaust Memorial Museum, which opened in 1993, included a film on the history of anti-Judaism in Europe. After the ELCA declaration was adopted, the museum added a note indicating that Lutherans in America had rejected Luther's recommendations.[2] Requested by a churchwide assembly and adopted by the Church Council, the declaration remains the primary official ELCA statement on Jewish-Lutheran relations.

In 1998, the panel produced "Guidelines for Lutheran-Jewish Relations."[3] These guidelines offer fifteen items of practical advice. In 2002, the panel released "Talking Points: Topics in Lutheran-Jewish Relations," a packet of discussion starters on eight topics. Each has a summary statement, a brief explanation of the topic, and questions for discussion. These eight discussion starters were followed in 2008 by a book with an explanatory chapter on each talking point, *Covenantal Conversations:*

---

1 http://download.elca.org/ELCA%20Resource%20Repository/Declaration_Of_The_ELCA_To_The_Jewish_Community.pdf.

2 The Lutheran Church–Missouri Synod, likely motivated by the 500th anniversary of Luther's birth, had already passed a resolution in 1983 deploring and disassociating itself from Luther's negative statements about the Jewish people. It, however, has abstained from any ongoing dialogue or cooperation with the Jewish community.

3 www.elca.org/en/Faith/Ecumenical-and-Inter-Religious-Relations/Inter-Religious-Relations/Jewish-Relations

Christians in Dialogue with Jews and Judaism[4] and by a DVD two years later with the same title. In the DVD, the author of each chapter in the book indicates how he or she became interested in Jewish-Lutheran relations, identifies one main point in the chapter, and explains its importance for a local congregation.

Anticipating the 500th anniversary of the Reformation, to be observed in 2017, the Consultative Panel on Lutheran-Jewish Relations has recently issued a four-page resource, "Why Follow Luther Past 2017? A Contemporary Lutheran Approach to Inter-Religious Relations."[5] The resource acknowledges that Luther's own statements about the Jews do not provide a model for today, but it goes on to suggest that some of his basic principles[6] can support inter-religious dialogue. Those principles include:

(1) God adopts people solely out of generosity, without prerequisites. This means that those of us who benefit from this generosity cannot know its limits. All we can do is to celebrate this reconciling generosity, share it, and embody it in our relations with others.

(2) In and through humans, God is active in the world. Whatever any human has, it comes from God. This means that the benefits of life, food, family, and community are not experienced only by one group. Although not everyone acknowledges God's gifting, this gifting provides a shared experience which can influence how Christians approach those who practice another religion.

> Faith lives with all sorts of unanswered questions. It is possible to relate to persons in another religion without knowing in advance how God regards that religion.

(3) Luther's "theology of the cross" limits our claims to know. This means that we need to be cautious about claiming too much

---

4 Edited by Darrell Jodock and published by Fortress Press.

5 http://download.elca.org/ELCA%20Repository/Why_Follow_Luther_Past_2017.pdf

6 A basic principle is not one belief alongside of other beliefs but an approach that influences how those beliefs are understood and interpreted.

certainty for any of our beliefs or ideas that goes beyond what has been revealed. To be sure, through revelation we *can* know God's attitude toward us and glimpse something of God's character and God's purpose, but faith depends on God's grace and lives with all sorts of unanswered or not-yet-answered questions. And this limit on our knowing means that we do not need to know in advance how God regards another religion in order to relate with generosity of spirit to persons in that religion. Though inter-religious dialogue usually deepens and strengthens one's own faith, it sometimes challenges one's ideas and beliefs about that faith. We should not be afraid of those challenges, because we are called to grow in faith and understanding, and growth involves change.

(4) Believers have a calling to serve the neighbor and the community. To do so, it is crucial that they listen to others, including those whose religion differs from their own. Indeed, if God's goal is shalom (whole, healthy relationships among humans, between God and humans, and between humans and the rest of creation), then our calling is relational. It involves initiating and building healthy, life-giving relationships, even when this means crossing boundaries and encountering the unfamiliar.

> Our calling is relational. It involves initiating and building healthy, life-giving relationships, even when this means crossing boundaries.

The overall purpose of "Why Follow Luther Past 2017" is to articulate a theological basis for engaging in inter-religious conversations and cooperative activities. It does not seek to answer all the questions that arise, such as "Who is saved?" or "What role do other religions play in God's plan for the world?" These are important questions, but best considered after we have experienced another religion and learned to understand it and its adherents. Some of the ready-made answers provided by our society are no longer viable. One such "answer" is the Deist "all religions are basically the same." The differences among religions are just too great for this to be credible. Another ready-made "answer" is the developmentalist "all other religions are relics of the past that have been superseded by Christianity." But the vitality of other religions and the moral accomplishments of some of their adherents are also too great for this to be self-evident. Formulating a workable outlook is an unfinished project, one to which every participant in inter-religious relations is invited to contribute.

We turn now to the Consultative Panel on Lutheran-Muslim Relations.[7] It has produced its own "Talking Points: Topics in Christian-Muslim Relations" with nine brief discussion starters. In cooperation with A Center of Christian-Muslim Engagement for Peace and Justice at the Lutheran School of Theology at Chicago (CCME), it has also produced a study guide for use with the six-disc DVD series, *Discover Islam*, produced by Discover Islam—USA and endorsed by the Islamic Society of North America. The guide provides an interpretive framework from a Christian point of view.[8]

TALKING POINTS

Topics in Christian-Muslim Relations

The Bible and the Qur'an

Jesus, Muhammed in the Qur'an

Law and Islam

Women in Islam

Forgiveness and Salvation

Caring for Creation

Practicing Hospitality

Believing in God

Walking Points

Looking back to the 1960s, a kind of trajectory can be seen. The decisions of Vatican Council II (1962-65) authorized Roman Catholics to join the ecumenical movement that had begun among Protestants in 1910. The result was a flurry of ecumenical dialogues, with relational and theological benefits the ELCA would later inherit. Moreover, both ongoing reflections on the Holocaust and *Nostra Aetate*, the path-breaking statement by Vatican II about non-Christian religions, spurred Jewish-Christian conversations. When the ELCA was formed in 1988, its Office of Ecumenical Affairs continued dialogues begun earlier and forged full-communion agreements with several Protestant churches, while at the same time recognizing the importance of dialogue with Jews and Judaism. As already mentioned, within a year a Consultative Panel on Lutheran-Jewish Relations was formed. After September 11, 2001, Lutheran-Muslim relations began to receive increased attention, and a Consultative Panel on Lutheran-Muslim Relations was added. Along with its ecumenical partner churches, the ELCA has recently expanded the focus on the Abrahamic traditions to the more inclusive "inter-religious relations." Most of the work with the non-Abrahamic religions is carried out through the National Council of Churches.

Today inter-religious conversations are happening at every level of the church—national, synodical (regional), and local. Recently new pro-

---

7 www.elca.org/en/Faith/Ecumenical-and-Inter-Religious-Relations/Inter-Religious-Relations/Muslim-Relations

8 More information is at http://elca.org/en/Faith/Ecumenical-and-Inter-Religious-Relations/Inter-Religious-Relations/Muslim-Relations.

grams have emerged on the ELCA college/university campuses, and a loose network has begun to form. Unlike congregations, these colleges/universities can draw on the diversity within their midst (with students, faculty, and staff of various backgrounds) as well as the diversity found in their surrounding communities. In addition, trained teachers and courses in other religions are readily available on campus. The colleges understand their calling as Lutheran institutions to include fostering inter-religious understanding as part of their contribution to the church and to society as a whole. As Concordia College has phrased it, the college "practices interfaith cooperation because of its Lutheran dedication. . . ." Over the years the ELCA colleges have provided congregations with a significant cadre of lay and rostered leaders. In the future, these leaders will have competency in inter-religious understanding and cooperation.

This Book: Its Origin and Purpose

During the first joint meeting of the two consultative panels in 2012, there was discussion with then-Presiding Bishop Mark S. Hanson about the theological and practical challenges of inter-religious engagement across the ELCA. The panelists decided to invite people in ELCA ministries throughout the nation to submit stories regarding their inter-religious experiences. Those who responded were free to describe what went well and/or to describe the difficulties encountered. Over fifty stories were received. The panels then decided to make them available to a larger audience, to provide some reflection on their content, and to synthesize the stories in four topical chapters. Thus this book came into being.

Its purpose is to encourage inter-religious conversations, both by providing examples of what others have tried and by suggesting reasons for initiating such conversations. The book grounds these reasons in the doctrine of vocation—that God calls everyone to be a neighbor, to love and serve other human beings. As the Parable of the Good Samaritan points out, the question is not "who is my neighbor?" (Luke 10:29, NRSV)—as if one can draw a line between who is and who is not—but "who is a neighbor to others?" (cf. Luke 10:36). The focus is on our behavior. Included among our neighbors are those of other religions. So, the basic question is: what does our calling, our vocation, mean with regard to how we treat those who practice other religions?

> This book's purpose is to encourage inter-religious conversations, both by providing examples of what others have tried and by suggesting reasons for initiating such conversations.

The conviction undergirding this book is that engaging the neighbor who practices a different religion is not only an avenue to good community relations, not only a way to learn things about those neighbors and their religion, but also an incentive to learn more about one's own faith. Some Americans have the impression that respect for other religions requires a lessened commitment to one's own faith. The conviction of this book is that the opposite is true. Deep commitments to the Christian faith and respect for those who practice other religions go hand in hand. A significant conversation with a person from another religion usually yields a desire for more information, not only about the other religion but also about one's own.

Often the road to mutual understanding can be bumpy. At some point a person is likely to find one's own beliefs challenged. This is to be expected. But the challenge is the kind that calls for a reshaping and deepening of one's understanding of the faith rather than expecting that faith itself be lessened or abandoned.

This book does not seek to provide theological answers to all of the issues that arise in inter-religious dialogue. It does not answer the question, "What is God's relationship to the other religions?" In fact, it may turn out that, given the differences among religions, there is no *one* answer to this question. In any case, differences among the religions need to be taken into account, even if they are not explored in any detail in this volume. The point of view expressed here is that these very real differences should not prevent us from treating all others as neighbors and engaging with them in conversation and cooperation.

Likewise, this book does not take a stand on whether religious diversity is a good thing. Instead, it merely recognizes the reality that religious diversity does exist and then offers suggestions for how Christians treat their religiously diverse neighbors.

It is important to note that the word "religion" has more than one meaning—some broader and some more specific. As used in this book, "religion" does not encompass everything that goes under this name. It refers to the major religions of the world and to those religions as they are understood by persons who are well informed about their teachings and practices. Thus, a white supremacist group in the hills of Idaho might claim to be Christian but would not be considered Christian by anyone who understood its basic claims. Likewise, though it might demand a religious-like loyalty, an intense political ideology does not in this book qualify as a religion.

This book has four chapters. In the first, Mark Swanson explores the pathway to the present. As one looks at the last twenty-five years, what has changed? In the second chapter Carol Schersten LaHurd explores the stories that were submitted. How are people responding to the religious diversity in their own communities? What possibilities do their responses suggest? Are there things to be learned from the experience of others? Jonathan Brockopp in the third chapter identifies a few of the questions that emerge from inter-religious contact and suggests that Christians are called to hold some ideas in tension. Holding ideas in tension is a venerable part of the Lutheran tradition, tracing its roots to Luther himself.[9] The fourth chapter makes use of Paul Rajashekar's experience growing up in India to identify some additional basic concerns. He suggests that a relational understanding of Christ provides a helpful perspective for understanding how a person can be both committed to Christ and ready to treat with respect those who practice other religions.

Persons with less experience in inter-religious dialogue and those whose chief interest is exploring what others are doing will want to start with the first two chapters. Others who have some experience and are most interested in thinking theologically about inter-religious conversation may want to skip to the third and fourth chapters. In any case, the chapters are designed both to fit into the book as a whole and to be useful on their own. Individuals and study groups may decide to focus on any of the chapters.

Though the authors of this book are Lutheran, it should not be viewed as an official statement of the ELCA. It draws together experiences and proposals for ways to understand the urgency of inter-religious understanding without seeking to formulate an officially authorized position. Developing such a position is an important task, but it is a task for another day.

This book also does not describe the beliefs and practices of other religions—not because this information is unimportant but because it is readily

---

9 Examples of such tensions or paradoxes in Luther's thought include his view that a believer is simultaneously justified (right with God) and a sinner, that God is both hidden and revealed, that believers are both free lords of all, subject to none, and dutiful servants of all, subject to all.

available elsewhere. Basic information about other religions can be found in a variety of places, including, for example, Theodore Ludwig's book, *The Sacred Paths: Understanding the Religions of the World* (Macmillan, 1989) or Roland E. Miller's introductory chapter in *Lutherans and the Challenge of Religious Pluralism*, edited by Frank Klos, C. Lynn Nakamara, and Daniel Martinson (Augsburg, 1990). Persons who begin to talk seriously with neighbors who practice another religion soon feel the need for additional information.[10] College professors and seminary professors who have studied other religions are well equipped to provide instruction and identify additional educational resources. We urge individuals and congregations and study groups to seek them out.

In addition to recognizing the differences among the other major religions of the world, this book recognizes that the relationship between Christianity and each of the other religions is different. Consider Judaism as an example. The degree of overlap between it and Christianity is distinctive. Jews and Christians study the same texts. Though ordered and interpreted differently, all of the Jewish Scriptures are included in the Christian Bible. In Romans 11, Paul affirms the ongoing validity of God's promises to the Jews. Except for questions raised by the Christian doctrine of the Trinity, Jews and Christians share the same concept of God. This is, of course, not the case with Buddhism or Hinduism, even though there are other things that Buddhism and Christianity have in common and other places where Christianity and Hinduism overlap. This book will not explore the different kinds of relationships that exist among the religions or make judgments about them. When it recommends ways of treating the people who practice other religions, it is not assuming that each of those religions has the same relationship to Christianity as do the others.

As already mentioned, Christian vocation is the foundation for what this book recommends. One contribution Martin Luther made to ecumenical Christianity was his insistence that every believer has a calling,

---

10 Note the experience of the Institute for Jewish-Christian Understanding at Muhlenberg College. Now twenty-six years old, one of its first programs was a series of "living-room dialogues," where approximately equal numbers of "ordinary" Jews and Christians gathered to discuss a brief introduction to a topic. The conversations began with life events and calendar events and how each group celebrated them and then moved on to more difficult topics, such as different views of Jesus. What emerged from those conversations was a request for more education, so the Institute organized "mini-courses," each taught by a team of Jewish and Christian theologians. Conversation prompted participants to want to find out more, both about the other religion and about their own.

a vocation, to serve the neighbor, and that this calling does not require withdrawal from the world. Rather it fosters engagement with the needs of individuals and communities who live in this world. Family life, work, and community service can all be venues in and through which the neighbor and the larger community can be served. In order to live out this vocation, a believer must know what the neighbor needs. Christians who intend to help sometimes fail to do so because they misunderstand their neighbors. Because understanding comes from engagement, our vocation calls us to seek out the neighbor and to discern together what will be of benefit. In a religiously diverse community or society, our actions need to be guided by a deep understanding of those whose religious outlook differs from our own.

Though the number of localities without religious diversity continues to decline, some church members do live in places without any significant presence of other religions, while others live in neighborhoods with a high degree of religious diversity. Each of these settings requires a slightly different response. But, in either case, "the neighbor" is not only the person next door or down the street. Our ideas and decisions and actions often affect persons who live in other neighborhoods, in other parts of our country, and in other parts of the world. So, whatever the make-up of our communities, we are all called to inter-religious engagement.

> Whatever the make-up of our communities, we are all called to inter-religious engagement.

The Lutheran tradition also offers a clear distinction between what God has revealed and what we would like to know but has not been revealed. Pondering the latter in the light of revelation has been left to us humans. For example, the Scriptures have no single teaching about the relationship between the people of the covenant and those who practice other religions. Some parts of the Bible provide a very positive view of other peoples and of God's relationship with them, even when they do not worship the God of the covenant. Other passages urge a strict separation between the people of the covenant and those around them. The Bible is clear that God demonstrates a profound, steadfast love for us and, as Christians believe, further gifts us with a redeemer, Jesus the Christ. But apparently God has left the door open for believers to figure out how to regard other religions. God has given us freedom to learn and to think and has called us to engage with others without our knowing in advance where this engagement will lead. In fact, if we knew the outcome, we could skip the hard work of conversation, of learning, and of re-formulating our ideas, but we are instead called to be hospitable to others and to learn from engaging them. The dual gifts of calling and freedom support the responsibility to engage, to learn, to think, and to speak with accuracy and charity about our neighbors. And together, this calling and this freedom invite us to work alongside others for the common good.

Why Practice Inter-Religious Dialogue and Cooperation?

The very last section of this book will try to summarize the book's answer to the following question: Why practice inter-religious dialogue and cooperation? In order to anticipate what will be said there and in order to invite readers to watch for these themes as they read through the next chapters, the final section of the conclusion is reproduced here. It offers the following reasons for inter-religious dialogue and inter-religious cooperation:

One is our calling to serve the neighbor. Getting to know the neighbor is crucial if we are to serve that person or that person's community.

Closely related to this is a second: Members of other religions are often harmed when stereotypes are allowed to circulate without objection or correction. Finding out enough to challenge misinformation contributes to the well-being of our neighbors and the well-being of society as a whole.

Third, a growing number of Americans describe themselves as spiritual but not religious. Most of them believe in God or in a spiritual being but are disillusioned with the church. The reasons are many, but one of them is its historical exclusivism. They have trouble believing that their non-Christian friends are total outsiders in God's kingdom and under divine condemnation. Just as Martin Luther saw God's hand at work even in challenges to the church (such as that posed by the Turks who were threatening to overrun Germany), so God's hand may be at work in this challenge. In the voices of the church's critics, God may be calling Christians to move beyond the triumphalism of claiming exclusive rights to the truth toward a more humble and open exploration patterned after the way of the cross. This does *not* mean saying that all religions are the same *or* that they are all paths to the same goal. *Nor* does it mean abandoning or lessening our commitment to the faith. It *does* mean reserving judgment and exploring whether we have something to learn from those whose religious outlook differs from our own.

Fourth, Christians are called to be peacemakers. With all of the forces in our world that fragment and divide peoples, inter-religious co-operation has the potential to bring them together.

A fifth reason is the benefit it can bring to the Christian, whose own understanding of faith is typically deepened and enhanced in the process.

And a sixth has to do with our calling to be good citizens. This reason may need some additional explanation. Christians in the United States live in a society that is pluralistic. Not only are all the major religions of the world represented here and not only are they all to be tolerated, but they all have the same constitutional standing with regard to the government. Pluralism means that none has a privileged position and that Christians should not expect the government to pass laws that favor Christians, even though they have historically been in the majority. It is instead the responsibility of every citizen—Christian, Muslim, Jewish, Hindu, Buddhist—to distinguish between what is good for the population as a whole and what is good for their particular group. The only way citizens can do this is to build relations with members of other religions so that they can sort out together what actually serves the common good.[11] Otherwise, how is one to know?

To take this one step further, there are contributions that religions, when they work together, can make to society as a whole. For example, they have a shared interest in religious freedom. They have a shared interest in human dignity. They have a shared interest in feeding the hungry, providing access to health care, and insuring economic opportunity for all. They have a shared interest in healthy families and healthy communities. Although sometimes it is forgotten as they fall victim to their own fear, they have a shared interest in fostering the wholeness of all humans and in all the conditions that make this possible. None of these shared goals can be attained in isolation or via religious conflict. Rather, the members of the various religions need to work together. And, if they do work together, they can have a much more credible influence on public policy than if they remain isolated. So, this sixth reason for engaging in inter-religious dialogue and cooperation is to be able to maximize the benefits Christians and others can contribute to society as a whole. There is little doubt that our fractured world needs their contribution.

---

11 Those who do not engage in these conversations often fear that Jews or Muslims want to take over the nation and reshape it. This fear is counter-productive. It creates the kind of unhealthy competition and distrust that undermines the goal of working together for the common good.

While recognizing that the road to inter-religious understanding can be a demanding pilgrimage with not all the theological questions settled in advance, the purpose of this book is to provide encouragement (theological and practical) to engage in respectful conversation and co-operation. I invite you to explore what it says.

FOR DISCUSSION

1. Regarding persons of another religion, this book seeks to ground our approach in the doctrine of vocation (that is, our calling to serve the neighbor and the community). Is this helpful? What are the implications for your life?

2. The Introduction says that believers do not need to know what God's attitude is toward another religion in order to treat its adherents with generosity and to witness to the generosity of God. Do you agree with this approach? Why or why not?

3. If shalom is all about relationships, and if God's goal is to foster shalom all around, how does this affect our understanding of the Christian faith and Christian discipleship?

4. What role does religion play in peacemaking? How can our own religion be an agent of peacemaking rather than an agent of conflict?

CHAPTER ONE

New Realities, New Thinking Since 1990

Mark Swanson

Introduction

The preacher of the biblical book of Ecclesiastes claims that "there is nothing new under the sun" (Ecclesiastes 1:9, NRSV). That is a rather sobering thought with which to begin a chapter about "new realities" of religious plurality in North America and the "new thinking" that these new realities have elicited from Christian teachers and preachers. New realities? The *fact* of the existence in North America of diverse examples of the complexes of belief, story, ritual, and life that we call "religions" is nothing new. European colonists (themselves a wildly diverse lot) encountered Native Americans and their richly diverse religious life. Enslaved Africans brought their religions, including Islam, to the New World. The Spanish trans-Pacific trade brought people as well as goods, including adherents of the ancient faiths of Asia. Waves of migration to the United States in the nineteenth and early twentieth centuries included, for example, European Jews, Lebanese and Bosnian Muslims, Chinese and Japanese Buddhists, as well as Christians of all sorts. The *fact* of religious diversity in the Americas, and in the United States of America in particular, is nothing new.

Still, the exposure of many North American Lutherans to religions other than Western forms of Christianity remained fairly limited until a few decades ago. Garrison Keillor's description of Lake Wobegon, with its Lutheran church, Catholic parish, and small conventicle of Sanctified Brethren, is a caricature—but a caricature makes us laugh precisely because its subject is recognizable. Many ELCA Lutherans today can remember communities where the major religious differences were between Lutherans and Catholics, or Lutherans and other Lutherans, or Lutherans and related Protestants. I think of a tiny town on the prairie where many of my own ancestors are buried, where the religious dividing line was between the Swedish-background Augustana Lutherans and the Swedish-background Evangelical Covenant tradition.

North American Lutherans were, from an early time, committed to global mission—so that the experience of the world's religions was especially that of *missionaries*. I remember from my own membership in a "junior missionary society" the visits of missionaries to Japan, China, India, and Tanzania. We learned something of the faiths of people on the other side of the world, even though my most vivid memories are of watching slide shows of exotic places and learning to sing "Jesus Loves Me" in Swahili and Chinese. It was only several years later that I became aware of missionaries who had become serious scholars of Islam (e.g., in India) or of Asian religions (e.g., in Hong Kong or Japan).

A major turning point for religious diversity in the United States was reached with the passage of the Immigration and Nationality Act of 1965 (the Hart–Celler Act), which abolished the (discriminatory) national quotas that had, for many decades, been a feature of U.S. immigration law, in favor of qualifications such as occupational skills and family already in the country. The act opened a door to new immigrants from Asia, Africa, and the Middle East—who brought their religions with them. If one visits large Islamic centers, Hindu and Buddhist temples, or Middle Eastern Christian churches in major U.S. cities today, one discovers that many of them were founded by new immigrants (and then new citizens) in the 1970s and 80s.

It was twenty-five years after the Hart–Celler Act, in 1990, that Augsburg Fortress Publishers published a volume of essays by Lutheran theologians called *Lutherans and the Challenge of Religious Pluralism.*[1] The timing was significant. The Evangelical Lutheran Church in America had come into existence just two years earlier, bringing together different histories of inter-religious encounter (through missionary work and domestic ministry) and theological reflection. Where did, or should, the newly-constituted denomination stand with regard to the "challenge" of religious difference—not only on the mission field but, increasingly over the previous quarter-century, in North American cities and towns? One of the volume's editors, Frank Klos, put the question this way:

> Lutherans in the United States and Canada are well aware
> that their societies have become multiracial, multi-lifestyle

---

1   Frank W. Klos, C. Lynn Nakamura, and Daniel F. Martensen, eds., *Lutherans and the Challenge of Religious Pluralism* (Minneapolis: Augsburg, 1990).

and multi religious. What does this mean for us as thoughtful, committed followers of Jesus Christ? How do we build friendly, healthy relationships with neighbors who have different faiths from our own?[2]

Reading these lines in 2015, one might be tempted to think that little has changed. The present book bears witness to the same awareness and struggles with the same questions! Has nothing changed in the past quarter century? Again, is there "nothing new under the sun"?

Many of our challenges indeed remain the same, and *Lutherans and the Challenge of Religious Pluralism* can still be read with great benefit. It gives basic instruction about the world's great religions, attempting to identify the "core or dominant intuition" of each;[3] studies the importance of community in Eastern religions;[4] inquires about other religions' attitudes towards Jesus Christ;[5] asks what it means for religious claims to be *true*;[6] and, finally, reflects on the kind of *dialogue* to which Lutheran Christians are called.[7] There is both useful instruction and provocative analysis to be found in these pages.

Still, there *have* been changes over the past quarter century. Inter-religious encounters hardly thought of in 1990 are now not at all uncommon. Consider, for example, a series of Sunday afternoon presentations that took place at a mosque in a Chicago suburb in the spring of 2014. The Lutheran School of Theology at Chicago and the Mosque Foundation North jointly sponsored a four-week course on "The Bible and the Qur'an," in which Christian professors taught about the Bible (and distinctive Christian beliefs), and a Muslim professor about the Qur'an (and distinctive Islamic beliefs), to a mixed body of Christians, Muslims, and others. A lot of time was allowed for conversation, during which participants discovered areas of profound agreement (e.g., that God's intention for human beings is that they should fulfill God's will with spontaneous joy and delight) *and* of profound difference (e.g., about how God has addressed the waywardness—or, in Christian terms, fallenness—of human beings). Both the agreements and the differences were vigorously but

---

2 Frank W. Klos, Preface, in Klos et al., v.

3 Miller, "Religion and Religions," Chapter 1 in Klos et al., *Lutherans and the Challenge of Religious Pluralism*.

4 Wi Jo Kang, "The Sense of Community in Asian Religions," Chapter 2 in Klos et al.

5 Carl E. Braaten, "The Identity and Meaning of Jesus Christ," Chapter 3 in Klos et al.

6 Paul R. Sponheim, "The Truth Will Make You Free," Chapter 4 in Klos et al.

7 Paul Varo Martinson, "What Then Shall We Do?" Chapter 5 in Klos et al.

respectfully discussed. Friendships were made and, over refreshments, ideas hatched for future shared Christian-Muslim projects.

This mini-course is just one example of scores of programs of its kind in recent years, in congregations, seminaries and colleges, schools and confirmation classes. At the University of Wisconsin in Madison, the Lubar Institute for the Study of the Abrahamic Religions, founded as a response to the 9/11 attacks, strives to raise up "leaders in the global and pluralistic world of tomorrow." Assistant Director (and ELCA pastor) Ulrich Rosenhagen reports that at monthly meetings, religiously diverse groups of students "discuss anything from high theology ('Are we worshipping the same God?') and religious practice ('How do you pray the Rosary?' 'How do you prostrate?' 'What do you do on your holiday?') to contested topics like the Danish Muhammad cartoons, or the stereotyping of Muslims and Jews in American pop culture." At Augustana College, Rock Island, student leaders of the Interfaith Understanding Group designed joint worship experiences that, with great sensitivity to the integrity of different faith traditions, provided an opportunity to reflect on common questions. At California Lutheran University, the Interfaith Allies sought to embed interfaith awareness throughout campus life. Examples can be multiplied of the way that ELCA seminaries and colleges have been addressing "the challenge of religious pluralism" with great creativity, sometimes in partnership with organizations such as the Interfaith Youth Core. But inter-religious exposure does not have to wait until the college years! Trinity Lutheran Seminary recently ran a Summer Sampler for high school students from Jewish, Muslim, and Christian backgrounds which opened, former director Laura Book reports, with a kosher dinner at the Main Street Orthodox Synagogue and an introduction to some ground rules for inter-religious dialogue, including: "This is a safe space; listen deeply, do not judge, and you must respect one another at all times." And when he was in parish ministry in Montana, ELCA pastor William Dohle invited nearby Rabbi Barbara Block to bring "her own wisdom and faith tradition to the table, in a brilliant presentation." That led to a confirmation class visit to the rabbi's synagogue.

It is perhaps examples like these that illustrate how our situation in 2015 differs from what it was in 1990. In *Lutherans and the Challenge of Religious Pluralism* there is a sense that the encounter with people of other faiths was, for most North American Lutherans (other than missionaries), a fairly *new* thing, requiring very basic instruction about world religions. Since then, at least in many congregations, we have moved a little beyond "World Religions 101." For the 1990 book, the experience of "religious pluralism" still feels like a mostly *foreign* phenomenon. Today, in many congregations, we've come to know our neighbors of other religions and have often visited their places of worship. And while *Lutherans and the Challenge of Religious Pluralism* warmly commends inter-religious dialogue, the book itself is largely a dialogue among Lutherans *about* encounter with people of other religions. Today, however, North American Lutherans—including our children and young adults—are more and more experiencing dialogue *with* people of other religions. We have listened to and shared with one another, have broken bread together, have reverently observed one another's worship, and have worked together in the service of our communities.[8]

Published in 1990, *Lutherans and the Challenge of Religious Pluralism* preceded the acceleration of immigration to the United States during the 1990s and the rate at which new religious communities are growing and maturing. While the writers of the book were not blind to realities of violence in the world, the book was published long before the al-Qaida attacks of September 11, 2001, or the outrages of other violence-glorifying cults like Boko Haram or Daesh (the self-declared "Islamic State"). It predated the media-amplified and politically-exploited fear and suspicion of religious others (Muslims in particular) that would become so common in the 2000s, on the one hand, *and* the simultaneous and intensive efforts by people of many faiths to create inter-religious understanding and solidarity, on the other. As a result, *Lutherans and the Challenge of Religious Pluralism* can sometimes sound a bit dated.[9] Roland E. Miller begins his introductory chapter by describing the religious diversity in an imaginary "Mainville, U.S.A.," where, he relates, "the *Mainville Daily Herald* announced the dedication of a new Muslim mosque!"[10] For readers who have experienced the controversies swirling around mosque-building in the United States, most notoriously the strident opposition in the summer of 2010 to a proposed Islamic community center in lower Manhattan (the so-called "Ground Zero Mosque" controversy), the notion that one could pick up one's newspaper and note almost in passing that "there's

---

8   On the various forms of dialogue, see the text box "Learning from the Roman Catholic Model" in Chapter Two, 49.

9   This is not a criticism. The book correctly, nearly prophetically, identified an issue that would be critical for the life of the church in the decades ahead.

10 Miller, "Religion and Religions," in Klos et al., 2.

a new mosque in town" seems a vestige of a more innocent age. North American Lutherans have not only been aware of the controversies surrounding efforts to build mosques and Islamic community centers, but sometimes they also have stood in solidarity with their Muslim neighbors and offered meaningful support.[11]

The *experience* of religious pluralism that North American Christians have gathered over the past quarter century has both resulted in and been sustained and nourished by *reflection. Should* we invest time in meeting and getting to know our neighbors of other faiths? If so, how can we do so as faithful disciples of Jesus Christ? What does the Bible, or the cumulative experience of the church, have to teach us? Here, practice leads to theological reflection, and theological reflection leads back to practice. Our efforts to behave as disciples of Jesus in a world of many religions raise questions that send us back to Scripture and Christian history. Our discoveries there may then redirect or provide renewed motivation for lives of discipleship in a religiously plural world.

In what follows, I suggest four areas in which, during these past years, Christians who have been reflecting on encounters with people of other religions have discovered wisdom in the Bible and in ancient Christian practices.[12] There is nothing radically "new under the sun" to be found here. Christians throughout history have striven to (1) speak the truth; (2) attend to the "outsider"; (3) pursue hospitality; and (4) seek deepened faith through pilgrimage. But in these last years, these four ancient themes, it seems to me, have been picked up, reflected upon, and put into practice in new and fresh ways.

1. Speaking Truth

Christians confess that "in the beginning was the Word, and the Word was with God, and the Word was God" (John 1:1, NRSV). Just so, words matter. The earliest Christian church knew this, and the careful, truthful use of words was, from the beginning, one of the marks of the Christian community. For example, in the letter to the Ephesians we read:

---

11 See Chapter Two, 74 ("Religious Neighbors Together—and Serving the World"), for an example of an ELCA congregation that helped to reverse a zoning commission's decision not to allow the building of a mosque in DuPage County, Illinois.

12 I should note that much of what I will present below has a North American, English-language focus (although I believe that it is relevant more widely). I also note that the theological conversations described here have been ecumenical from the start, although ELCA Lutherans have regularly participated in them (as I hope will become apparent from some of the examples).

So then, putting away falsehood, let all of us speak the truth to our neighbors, for we are members of one another (Ephesians 4:24, NRSV).

This and similar New Testament exhortations are related to a much older commandment, concerning not only speech *to* but also speech *about* the neighbor:

You shall not bear false witness against your neighbor (Exodus 20:16; Deuteronomy 5:20, NRSV).

What does it mean to follow this eighth commandment[13] in a world in which we are inundated with words and in which we can so easily, in so many different media, add to the flood? This is a serious question for Christians, who attempt to be alert to the ways in which the tongue can be "a restless evil, full of deadly poison," with which one can "bless the Lord and Father" but also "curse those who are made in the likeness of God" (James 2:8-9, NRSV). All too often, the poison of the tongue (as well as of words written and digitized) has been directed against non-Christians. The Christian community's history of anti-Jewish speech goes back to its beginnings. In recent years we have experienced a surge of anti-Islamic discourse, ranging from scholarly-sounding analyses to careless generalizations to out-and-out falsehoods and slanders.[14] Such speech does not exist in a vacuum; it seeks to grab people's attention (and stir up righteous outrage) in a quest for celebrity or media market share or political support.

In the midst of swamps of poisoned words—not only about people on the basis of their religious beliefs but also on the basis of race, sexual orientation, or political affinities—Christians have been struck anew by the Bible's call to be speakers of truth. Martin Luther's explanation of the eighth commandment in the Small Catechism is particularly relevant for thinking about our calling in a multi-religious world:

We are to fear and love God, so that we do not tell lies about our neighbors, betray or slander them, or destroy their reputations.

---

13 Or ninth commandment, depending on how one is counting. Lutherans know it from the Small Catechism as the eighth commandment.

14 The invented claim that verse 9:11 of the Qur'an spoke of the "wrath of the eagle in the lands of Allah" was eagerly picked up and circulated on the internet, before being debunked. More disturbing than such hoaxes-gone-viral is the seemingly learned "analysis" that claims that scholarly Muslims who emphasize the Qur'an's verses of tolerance are intentionally lying (about verses they know well to have been "abrogated"). This "analysis" is at once scholarly-sounding (complete with explanations of Arabic legal terms), generalizing (by claiming this to be generally true of educated Muslims), and just plain slanderous. It continues to have a life on the internet (as a search under the terms *taqiyya* and *naskh* will quickly reveal).

Instead we are to come to their defense, speak well of them, and interpret everything they do in the best possible light.[15]

How shall this be done? The examples mentioned above and throughout this book are instructive. They all gave participants the opportunity to "get the other straight"—that is, to ask questions, to listen, to learn, to overcome stereotypes and suspicions, and even to more fully understand one's own tradition. But more than that, they all provided the opportunity for the building of relationships, to *make friends*. I can think of no greater help and incentive for inter-religious truth-telling than having friends of other faiths.[16] I become more sensitive to stereotypes and unfair generalizations *because they are not true of my friends*. I may be moved to stand up to spreaders of falsehood *in defense of my friends*. When I need more information, I will *have trusted friends to whom I may turn*. And when I misspeak, *my friends may set me straight*.

Sometimes the misspeaking may require soul-searching, contrition, and the seeking of forgiveness. Martin Luther was one of the greatest interpreters of the eighth commandment. However, Luther himself did not always follow his own rules. As he became more and more aware of the devil's work in the world, he became more and more willing to identify his opponents with that work. The pope and his apologists, the Protestant theological opponents whom Luther called "*Schwaermer*," and the Turks received scant courtesy from Luther. But Luther was at his very worst in his 1543 treatise, *Of the Jews and their Lies*. Sickeningly painful to read today (the destruction of synagogues and schools was but the first in a series of "remedial" actions that Luther recommended), Luther's treatise was deplored by both friends and opponents but periodically rediscovered, including by both late nineteenth-century anti-Semites and Nazis who wanted to claim Luther's legacy in the 1930s and 40s.[17]

---

15 Martin Luther, The Small Catechism, in *The Book of Concord: The Confession of the Evangelical Lutheran Church*, ed. Robert Kolb and Timothy J. Wengert (Minneapolis: Fortress Press, 2000), 353.

16 One of North American Lutheranism's teachers in Christian-Muslim relations, the Rev. Dr. Roland E. Miller, entitled his introduction to Islamic faith and practice *Muslim Friends: Their Faith and Feeling* (St. Louis: Concordia Publishing House, 1996). He reminds his readers from the beginning that to come to know another religious tradition is to make friends with living and breathing, believing and emoting people. Another one of our teachers in Christian-Muslim relations, the Rev. Dr. Harold Vogelaar, cultivated inter-religious friendships on three continents.

17 For a brief introduction, see Heiko A. Oberman, *Luther: Man between God and the Devil*, Image Books Edition (New York and London: Image–Doubleday, 1992), 292-97 ("Darkness at Noon: Luther and the Jews"). For a recent collection of texts by two Gettysburg Seminary professors, see *Martin Luther, The Bible, and the Jewish People: A Reader*, ed. Brooks Schramm and Kirsi I. Stjerna (Minneapolis: Fortress Press, 2012).

If that was Luther at his worst, however, the ELCA was at its best in its 1994 "Declaration of the Evangelical Lutheran Church in America to the Jewish Community."[18] Drawing on a similar declaration made by the Lutheran World Federation in 1982,[19] this was an act of truth-telling and repentance that was widely appreciated within the Jewish community in the United States and which opened the way to deeper relationships.

Can we learn to speak about our neighbors in ways that they themselves recognize as generous and truthful to themselves and their faith? The greatest saints of inter-religious dialogue have devoted much of their lives to just that: learning to speak of that which the neighbor regards as holy in a way that the neighbor may find not only accurate, but also perhaps even beautiful and eye-opening, expressing and creating what the late Lutheran bishop and professor Krister Stendahl used to call "holy envy."[20] One of my own first mentors in Islamic studies, Professor Willem Bijlefeld of Hartford Seminary, had traveled extensively throughout "the Muslim world," giving lectures on what he as a Christian had heard in the Qur'an. Muslims in his audiences were often moved and sometimes asked him how it could be that he had not yet converted to Islam! The act of generous and appreciative description was an act of Christian love. Even more, it provided an occasion for and invitation to deep conversation and mutual witness.

2. Attentiveness to the "Outsider"

The Christian church is a community that reads the Holy Scripture, turning to it for guidance as it encounters new challenges. Over the past quarter century, as churches have wrestled with various issues of inclusion, and perhaps especially in the context of debates about immigration and about Christian attitudes towards non-Christians, a remarkable set of stories have almost leapt off Scripture's pages. Let's call them "outsider stories," in which the one who brings help and blessing or who speaks necessary truth is someone from *outside* the immediate circle of ethnicity, kinship, and faith.

---

18 See more in the Introduction, "Time-Tested Questions," 13.

19 For the documents of Christian-Jewish dialogue, see the collection of Lutheran seminary and college professor Franklin Sherman, *Bridges: Documents of the Christian-Jewish Dialogue*, 2 vols. (New York and Mahwah, New Jersey: Paulist Press, 2011-2014). The 1982 LWF statement is at 1:142-51.

20 See, for example, Yehezkel Landau, "An Interview with Krister Stendahl," *Harvard Divinity Bulletin* 35.1 (Winter 2007), online at http://bulletin.hds.harvard.edu/articles/winter2007/interview-krister-stendahl

At the Chapel of the Incarnation, Luther Seminary, one day in 2002, Prof. Terry Fretheim preached a homily on a passage of Scripture that we seldom hear read in church: Genesis 20, on the sojourn of Abraham and Sarah in Gerar. It is hard to portray "Father" Abraham in a good light in this passage: Fearing for his own life, he passes off his beautiful and desirable wife Sarah as his sister—and almost inevitably she is claimed and "taken" by King Abimelech. When God in a dream tells Abimelech that he has committed a mortal sin by taking another man's wife, he reproaches Abraham: "You have done things to me that ought not to be done. . . . What were you thinking of, that you did this thing?" (Genesis 20:9-10, NRSV). Fretheim pointed out that in this passage it is the *outsider* who receives a revelation from God, who speaks truth, and who, in fact, becomes teacher and confessor to "insider" Abraham.[21]

Such "outsider stories" are by no means rare in Scripture. King Abimelech provides just one example of the role of outsiders in the Bible's Abraham narrative (as Fretheim carefully shows in his book, *Abraham: Trials of Family and Faith*).[22] The New Testament is full of "outsider stories," beginning with Matthew 2[23] and the story of the Magi—astrologers from the East (of all people!) who made a dangerous journey, bearing gifts, in order to pay homage to the one born "King of the Jews." Perhaps pride of place among biblical "outsider stories" belongs to the Parable of the Good Samaritan (Luke 10:29-37), which makes several appearances in this volume.[24] As we read these stories, we are impressed at the number of times that, in the Bible, it is someone from outside the community of "insiders" who brings blessing, hospitality, practical help, or (as in Abimelech's case) a true word of rebuke. Perhaps, as we read, the Holy Spirit is working through Scripture to shape us as people who are *attentive* to those outside our immediate communities, willing to learn from them and willing to accept the gifts they bring.

Christians have not always welcomed this work of the Spirit. Throughout much of Christian history, interpreters of these "outsider stories"

---

21 A summary of the main points of the homily may be found in Terence E. Fretheim, "Conversation or Conversion? Hearing God from the Other," *World & World* 22 (2002): 304, 306, online at http://wordandworld.luthersem.edu/content/pdfs/22-3_Conversion_Conversation/22-3_Face_to_Face.pdf.

22 Terence E. Fretheim, *Abraham: Trials of Family and Faith* (Columbia, South Carolina: The University of South Carolina Press, 2007). Chapters four through six deal with Abraham and outsiders.

23 Actually, we could begin with Matthew 1 and note the place of the Moabitess Ruth (verse 5) in the genealogy of the Messiah.

24 See especially Chapter Three, 90.

have tried to make the outsiders into insiders! For example, "outsider stories" have regularly been interpreted as symbolic stories or allegories, not to be read literally. If, in Genesis 20, Sarah can be made into a symbol of *virtue*, then Abraham's "sharing" of his wife with King Abimelech can become a story about how a righteous person does not keep virtue to himself![25] Throughout the history of the church, the Good Samaritan has been regarded as a symbol of Christ;[26] in fact, in some ancient pictures he even gets Christ's special cross-imbedded halo.[27] Another way of dealing with "outsiders" in Scripture was to create back-stories for them so as to make them less unfamiliar and strange. Just so, the mysterious magi or astrologers from the East of Matthew 2 gradually, through imaginative exegesis and the accumulation of legends, became the three beloved kings of art and Christmas pageants: Balthasar, Caspar, and Melchior.[28]

If, however, we can refrain from the temptation to "tame" the texts of Scripture and allow them to be mysterious and their characters strange, just so we may come to see that Scripture is spanned by an arc of stories[29] in which God uses people from outside the insiders' tightly-knit assemblies in order to challenge and to bless. Perhaps we will come to see these stories as not exceptional, but rather as profoundly relevant for the way that Christians can live in this world: attentive to outsiders, ready to be surprised by the ways in which God works in the world.

And, perhaps, ready to be transformed. One "outsider story" that has received renewed attention in these past years is that of Jesus' encounter with the Canaanite woman in Matthew 15:21-28. If we resist the tempta-

---

25 So said Origen of Alexandria in the third century: Origen, *Homilies on Genesis and Exodus*, translated by Ronald E. Heine (Washington, D.C.: The Catholic University of America Press, 1982), 122-23.

26 See François Bovon, *Luke 2: A Commentary on the Gospel of Luke 9:51–19:27*, translated by Donald S. Deer, Hermeneia (Minneapolis: Fortress Press, 2013), 60-64. Also for Luther, the Samaritan was Christ.

27 See the illustration of the story in the sixth-century Rossano Gospels manuscript: https://commons.wikimedia.org/wiki/File:RossanoGospelsFolio007vGoodSamaritan.jpg .

28 See Ulrich Luz, *Matthew 1-7: A Commentary*, trans. James E. Crouch, Hermeneia (Minneapolis: Fortress Press, 2007), 101-16 (esp. 115-16); Hans-Ruedi Weber, *Immanuel: The Coming of Jesus in Art and the Bible* (Grand Rapids, Michigan: Wm. B. Eerdmans Publishing Co.; Geneva: World Council of Churches, 1984), 70-72. ("Once the Magi were identified as kings, Christian imagination worked overtime," 70.)

29 Of course, the Bible is a big and complicated book, which also includes stories like, for example, the encounter of Elijah and the prophets of Baal (1 Kings 18), which ends in a massacre. Underlying this section is the assumption that the "arc of stories" described here is more definitive of Scripture as a whole, which is a story of divine hospitality—on which, see the next section.

tion to "tame" the story,[30] it is really quite shocking: Jesus ignores the pleas of the Canaanite woman, tells his disciples that he was "sent only to the lost sheep of the house of Israel," and then answers her direct appeal in a shockingly disrespectful way: "It is not fair to take the children's food and throw it to the dogs" (v. 26, NRSV)! But the woman, undeterred, responds, "Yes, Lord, yet even the dogs eat the crumbs that fall from their masters' table" (v. 27, NRSV). Jesus praises her faith and heals her daughter.[31] Could it be that in this story it was the Canaanite woman—the "outsider"—who was the teacher, and that Jesus learned from her, with the result that his mind was changed and his heart widened? If such an encounter can change Jesus, what about *us*?

Human beings find it difficult to allow those different from themselves to *be* different. The temptation is to eradicate or marginalize them, change them to be "like us," or define away the differences—deciding that "deep down" we're all really the same anyway. We have seen that it has even been difficult for readers of Scripture to allow "outsiders" to *remain* outsiders: remember how the Good Samaritan has regularly been made into Jesus! But perhaps, if we can avoid these temptations, Scripture's "outsider stories" point us towards a way of living with difference that is attentive, hopeful of blessing, and transformative in life-giving ways.

3. Pursuing Hospitality

I am writing these words during the Muslim month of Ramadan, when pious Muslims fast from all food and drink from first light until sunset. Ramadan has always been a month of *hospitality* in Islamic tradition. "Tables of the Merciful" are set up in cities and towns throughout the Islamic world, where everyone—rich and poor, neighbor and stranger—is welcome to stop and break the fast at sunset. Especially since 2001 in North America, such fast-breaking or *iftar* meals have become a place of mutual hospitality between Muslims, Christians, Jews, and other. Non-Muslims have hosted *iftar* meals for their Muslim neighbors, and Muslim communities have hosted interfaith *iftars* for *their* neighbors. Many North American Lutheran Christians have had their first experience in a specifically Islamic space by being a guest at a Ramadan *iftar*.

---

30 E.g., by claiming that Jesus knew the course of the conversation in advance, and was really "testing" the woman, or other ways of taking the sting out of Jesus' word about taking the children's food and throwing it to the dogs. See Roy A. Harrisville, "The Woman of Canaan: A Chapter in the History of Exegesis," *Interpretation* 20 (1966): 274-87, especially 281-83.

31 In Matthew's Gospel, the other person whose faith was praised by Jesus was another outsider: the centurion of Matthew 8:5-13. The disciples, by contrast, are often "You of little faith"!

As North American Christians have encountered neighbors from other faith traditions,[32] they have experienced and practiced hospitality—at seder celebrations, various kinds of community gatherings, reciprocal visits of worship spaces, *iftars*—learning to be good guests and good hosts.[33] While the giving and receiving of hospitality is nothing new, what is striking to me, looking back over the past quarter century, is the way that hospitality has been rediscovered as a major *theme* of Scripture, church history, and theological reflection. Two books by Episcopal priests were (for this writer, at least) forerunners of this trend: John Koenig's *New Testament Hospitality: Partnership with Strangers as Promise and Mission* (1985)[34] and Rowan Greer's *Broken Lights and Mended Lives* (1986), which includes an important chapter on hospitality in the early church.[35] Some time passed[36] before the publication of Christine Pohl's aptly titled *Making Room: Recovering Hospitality as a Christian Tradition* (1999),[37] but then the flood gates were open, and many English-language books have appeared with "hospitality" in the title.[38]

---

32 For more stories of hospitality and shared meals, see Chapter Two, 53.

33 Practical guides for being a good inter-religious guest exist, e.g. Arthur J. Magida, ed., *How to Be a Perfect Stranger: A Guide to Etiquette in Other People's Religious Ceremonies*, 2 vols. (Woodstock, Vermont: Jewish Lights Publishing, 1996-1997). However, being a good guest involves skills and attitudes beyond those that can be captured in a manual, that can only be gained by practice.

34 John Koenig, *New Testament Hospitality: Partnership with Strangers as Promise and Mission* (Philadelphia: Fortress Press, 1985). Note that it was a Lutheran press that published this pioneering work.

35 Rowan A. Greer, *Broken Lights and Mended Lives: Theology and Common Life in the Early Church* (University Park and London: Pennsylvania State University Press, 1986), Chapter 5.

36 I apologize for what I am sure are important omissions here!

37 Christine Pohl, *Making Room: Recovering Hospitality as a Christian Tradition* (Grand Rapids, Michigan: William B. Eerdmans Publishing Company, 1999).

38 Some examples: Brendan Byrne, *The Hospitality of God: A Reading of Luke's Gospel* (Collegeville, Minnesota: Liturgical Press, 2000); Amy G. Oden, ed., *And You Welcomed Me: A Sourcebook on Hospitality in Early Christianity* (Nashville: Abingdon Press, 2001); Luke Bretherton, *Hospitality as Holiness: Christian Witness Amid Moral Diversity* (Aldershot, U.K. and Burlington, Vermont: Ashgate, 2006); Arthur Sutherland, *I Was a Stranger: A Christian Theology of Hospitality* (Nashville: Abingdon Press, 2006); Elizabeth Newman, *Untamed Hospitality: (The Christian Practice of Everyday Life): Welcoming God and Other Strangers* (Grand Rapids, Michigan: Brazos Press, 2007); Amy G. Oden, *God's Welcome: Hospitality for a Gospel-Hungry World* (Cleveland: The Pilgrim Press, 2008); Letty M. Russell, *Just Hospitality: God's Welcome in a World of Difference*, ed. J. Shannon Clarkson and Kate M. Ott (Louisville: Westminster/John Knox Press, 2009); Maria Poggi Johnson, *Making a Welcome: Christian Life and the Practice of Hospitality* (Eugene, Oregon: Cascade Books, 2011); Fr. Daniel Homan, OSB, and Loni Collins Pratt, *Radical Hospitality: Benedict's Way of Love* (Brewster, Massachusetts: Paraclete Press, 2011).

Hospitality was being rediscovered as a major theme in Scripture, encompassing the creation (as the Triune God's gracious "making room" for and entering into relationship with human creatures); incarnation (as the Word came into the world as guest, seeking those who would receive him, John 1:12); Jesus' eating and drinking, or giving to eat and drink; or the sayings and parables in which God is portrayed as the host at a banquet. Beyond Scripture, hospitality continues as a major theme in the history of Christian life, from the hospitality practiced by early house churches to that of desert hermits to the fifty-third chapter of the *Rule* of St. Benedict, which opens: "All guests who present themselves are to be welcomed as Christ."[39]

Hospitality can become a specifically theological and missiological theme as well: The Triune God is hospitable, and the church's participation in the *missio Dei* (the mission of God) is a participation in the divine hospitality. That is, the church's practice of hospitality is anchored in the hospitality of *God*, and this practice of hospitality is not *in addition to* being in mission, but intrinsic to it.[40]

The recent burst of interest in hospitality as a biblical, church historical, theological, and ecumenical theme has much to do with our present U.S. American social, political, and ecclesial contexts. The theme has proved helpful for thinking about Christian life and mission in the midst of bewildering diversity and ongoing struggles to be inclusive of all God's children. Furthermore, the theme has provided help in thinking about major social issues such as immigration,[41] *and* it has been useful in thinking about possibilities for respectful and fruitful encounters with people of other religions. Here, the Apostle Paul's exhortation in Romans 12:13-14 seems especially relevant:

> Contribute to the needs of the saints;
> extend hospitality to strangers.
> Bless those who persecute you; bless and do not curse them (NRSV).

---

39 RB 1980: *The Rule of St. Benedict in English*, ed. Timothy Fry (Collegeville, Minnesota: The Liturgical Press, 1982).

40 See my own modest contribution to this literature: Mark N. Swanson, "Commending Hospitality and 'Polishing the Theologian in Us': Reflections on Theological Education for Mission," in *News of Boundless Riches: Interrogating, Comparing, and Reconstructing Mission in a Global Era*, 2 vols., ed. Lalsangkima Pachuau and Max L. Stackhouse (Delhi: ISPCK, 2007), 2:236-49. Note that here hospitality helps to define what mission is: God's hospitable (and not manipulative or coercive) embrace of human beings.

41 Two leaders in the ELCA wrote a book about hospitality in the context of a response to immigration: Stephen Bouman and Ralston Deffenbaugh, *They Are Us: Lutherans and Immigration* (Minneapolis: Fortress Press, 2009).

One way of reading this text is that the "strangers" to whom hospitality is to be extended fall *in between* "the saints" of the first line and the persecutors of the third. That is, these "strangers" are (or at least include) people who do not belong to the Christian community, but who are not persecuting it. Our non-Christian neighbors fall here—and the apostle's exhortation to the Christian community with respect to them is elegant in its brevity: "Extend hospitality." Or, translating Paul's Greek yet more literally than does the NRSV: "*Pursue* hospitality." Hospitality is not simply to be extended (which can be done grudgingly); possibilities for it are to be eagerly sought out. How can we offer others our friendship? How can we "make room" for them—in literal spacial terms (space to live, space to pray, space to park a car)—or at the tables where we discuss our future together, or in our hearts and imaginations?

As North American Christians have attended to the theme of hospitality, they have learned that genuine hospitality is *mutual*. So it was in the ministry of Jesus, in which the roles of guest and host alternate and flow one into the other. Jesus eats with tax collectors and sinners—and feeds the multitudes. He is a guest in the home of Mary and Martha—and Mary receives "the better part" served up by Jesus (Luke 10:38-42). He accepts the hospitality of the disciples on the road to Emmaus—and his identity is revealed as he gives thanks and breaks the bread (Luke 24:28-31, NRSV). This is important! There are too many instances in the world where the language of hospitality is abused, where power-wielding "hosts" remind others (immigrants and refugees, or "recent" arrivals from only a century or so back) that they are "only" guests. In true hospitality, one practices being both host *and* guest—sometimes simultaneously!

For many North American Lutherans, going out into the world of the religions *as a guest* is hard. Many of us are people of considerable privilege in the world and are enculturated to expect having some degree of *control*. In many ways, being host is easier than being a guest: One is serving one's own menu in one's own space according to one's own plan! But like Abraham setting off looking for those who would bless him (Genesis 12:3) or Jesus sitting at a well in Samaria waiting for someone to give him a drink (John 4:5ff.), the practice of mutual hospitality puts us in places where we are not in control, where we do not know what will happen next, where we need to be taught how to behave, where we depend upon others for our well-being. For Christians, though, there should not be anything strange about this. We practice being grateful guests at every eucharist, as we approach the Lord's table as guests, with empty hands.[42]

4. Pilgrimage (by Way of "Theologies Of Religions")[43]

At the time that *Lutherans and the Challenge of Religious Pluralism* was published, English-speaking theological students had for some years been learning the words *exclusivism, inclusivism*, and *pluralism* (and their corresponding *–ist* adjectives) in order to make some sense of what Christian theologians had taught about other religions.[44] According to this typology (and oversimplifying), a theology that proclaimed that a person may not be saved apart from an explicit confession of faith in Jesus Christ was *exclusivist*. A Christ-centered theology that could still somehow make room for God to save non-Christians was *inclusivist*. And a theology that saw different religions as different paths towards the same salvation was *pluralist*.

This three-fold typology was useful for sorting different theological positions held through the ages, but it quickly showed its limitations. Its use was seldom simply descriptive; rather, theologians used the typology as a (blunt) tool for arguing for what they thought to be the *right* position. Some teachers saw the three positions as ascending steps in inter-religious maturity, with *pluralist* understandings as the goal. Others sought to find the truth between two extremes, so that a generous but faithful *inclusivism* was the correct posture, avoiding the extremes of "fundamentalist" exclusivism and "relativist" pluralism.[45] The labels turned out to be quite slippery; theologians wanting to claim one or the other of the labels for a constructive project had to (re)define precisely what they meant by them.[46]

---

42 On being a guest in the world, see Chapter Four, 156.

43 While the term "theology/ies of religions" is a common one (see the references to Race and Knitter below), some of the authors in this volume prefer "theology/ies of religious plurality."

44 Alan Race, *Christians and Religious Pluralism: Patterns in the Christian Theology of Religions* (London: SCM Press, 1983).

45 A thoughtful critique of the usual ways of using the threefold typology is that of Michael Barnes, "Religious Pluralism" in *The Routledge Companion to the Study of Religion*, ed. John R. Hinnells (Abingdon, U.K.: Routledge, 2005), 407-22, especially 418. For Barnes, the three positions best represent the virtues or values of particular communities as they encounter religious others. I am grateful to Dr. Peter Pettit for bringing this essay to my attention.

46 Thus Diana L. Eck of the Pluralism Project at Harvard University claimed the words "pluralism" and "pluralist" for her own concerns and defined them especially in terms of praxis. See the page "What is pluralism?" at "The Pluralism Project at Harvard University," http://pluralism.org/pluralism/what_is_pluralism; or Diana L. Eck, *Encountering God: A Spiritual Journey from Bozeman to Banaras* (Boston: Beacon Press, 1993), especially Chapter Seven.

In any event, during the past quarter century we have learned that the variety of Christian reflection about religious plurality cannot be sorted into just three file folders. In 2002, Catholic theologian Paul Knitter redefined and renamed the just-mentioned categories (exclusivist, inclusivist, pluralist) as the *replacement, fulfillment*, and *mutuality* models, and then added a fourth, which he called the *acceptance* model.[47] This new category included the teachings of theologians who stressed the real *differences* between the religions. They cautioned that Christians shouldn't assume that they can know in advance what is going on in another religion.[48] These theologians often argue that different religions are rather like different languages. Inter-religious dialogue, while not impossible, will take a lot of listening and learning, time and patience.[49]

Knitter was also able to report on a movement called "comparative theology," which *begins* with this careful dialogue and puts the typologies (three-fold, four-fold, or whatever) aside.[50] These "comparative theologians" strive to be faithful in their own Christianity and then, without pre-judgments about what God might be doing in another religion, seek to learn something about that religion in the deepest way possible—and then see what happens. Rather than "doing theology" first and then asking about the consequences for dialogue, they call for the dialogue *first*. One ELCA Lutheran who has taken up this call is Gettysburg Seminary professor Kristin Johnston Largen, who built dialogue into the heart of Christian theological instruction in her book *Finding God among Our Neighbors*.[51] What better way (for example) to explore Christianity's unique (and often misunderstood) understanding of God as both one and triune than to bring it into conversation with, say, Islam's "pure monotheism" or Hinduism's understanding of "one and many"?[52] One image that has been proposed for doing "inter-religious theology" in this way is that of

---

47 Paul F. Knitter, *Introducing Theologies of Religions* (Maryknoll, New York: Orbis Books, 2002).

48 For example, "exclusivist" theologies sometimes claim to know that the non-Christian religions are merely human striving; "inclusivist" theologies may claim to know that the grace of Christ is mysteriously at work to bring non-Christians to a Christian fulfilment; or some "pluralist" theologies may claim to know that all religions are, at some deep level, about the same realities or headed towards the same goals.

49 Knitter begins his section on the "Acceptance Model" by summarizing material from North American Lutheran theologian George A. Lindbeck, in his book, *The Nature of Doctrine: Religion and Theology in a Postliberal Age* (Philadelphia: The Westminster Press, 1984); Knitter, *Introducing Theologies of Religions*, 178-85.

50 Knitter, *Introducing Theologies of Religions*, 202-14.

51 Kristin Johnston Largen, *Finding God among Our Neighbors: An Interfaith Systematic Theology* (Minneapolis: Fortress Press, 2013).

52 Ibid., 144-50.

pilgrimage: The pilgrim has a particular vocation in a particular place, but then leaves that place in order to seek out new encounters (with God, with human beings) in some other place. The pilgrim does not (usually) remain in the place of pilgrimage, however, but returns home, often as a changed person who brings renewal to the original community in surprising ways.[53] Can we, similarly, understand our encounters with people of other religions as a kind of pilgrimage, a journey to some special place where we anticipate that God will surprise and move us, and from which (as we return "home" to Christian ways of thinking and being in the world) we may find ourselves transformed?

Precisely this kind of understanding was suggested, at least for the "Abrahamic" (Christian-Muslim-Jewish) dialogue, by then-Lutheran World Federation President and ELCA Presiding Bishop Mark S. Hanson in October 2007, in a public response to a letter from world Muslim leaders entitled "A Common Word between Us and You."[54] The Muslim scholars' letter, which they addressed to Christian leaders around the world,[55] called for renewed engagement and understanding between Muslims and Christians around shared commitment to the fundamental commandments: love of God and love of the neighbor. Hanson's response included the following memorable lines:

> I acknowledge this letter in gratitude and recognition of the need for its further study and consideration. I likewise accept it in the belief that Jews, Muslims, and Christians are called to one another as to a holy site, where God's living revelation in the world is received in reverence among the faithful and not in fear of our neighbors.[56]

The metaphor of pilgrimage "to a holy site" is evocative in a number of ways. It draws out themes that we have already considered: expectation of blessing, even transformation, in anticipated encounters and experiences, and relying on the hospitality of others. And it adds others. Pilgrimage takes time. It is demanding. It requires commitment. But, if

---

53 For a beautiful exploration of this image, see A. Bagus Laksana, "Comparative Theology: Between Identity and Alterity," in *The New Comparative Theology: Inter-religious Insights from the Next Generation*, ed. Francis X. Clooney (London and New York: T&T Clark, 2010), Chapter One.

54 The full text of the letter, lists of signatories, and responses are all available at "A Common Word," www.acommonword.com/

55 Bishop Hanson was addressed in his capacity as President of the Lutheran World Federation.

56 www.acommonword.com/response-from-bishop-rev-mark-s-hanson/

we listen to Christians who have gone on pilgrimages to Jerusalem or Compostella, Muslims who have gone on pilgrimage to Mecca, or Hindus who have gone to Varanasi or Tirupathi, we hear that the rewards are great. The time, hardship, and commitment often lead not only to new insight, but also renewed life.

Perhaps our pilgrimage "to one another as to a holy site" is not so different from this. To think of our inter-religious engagement as pilgrimage reminds us that fruitful engagement requires more than a meal or a field trip or a class, as valuable as these things are. To achieve the sort of understanding that makes a difference *takes time and commitment*. There will be stumbles, misunderstandings, and decisions to continue despite difficulties. But the rewards are great: We rejoice in new friendships which will come to bear good fruit in our communities. We are grateful for every new insight, we will gain deeper understanding of our own faith, and we will learn to share it in simple words of genuine conviction. And along the way, we put our trust in the Triune God, who grasps and loves us, our friends of other religions, and the whole of creation.

Conclusion

The suggestions made above amount to a kind of proposal for how Christians can live in a world of many religions. In the first place, we can live as faithful Christians! Nothing in what has been said calls for those of us who are Christians to compromise our discipleship to Jesus Christ. Rather, the question is about *how* to live out this discipleship.

How? Over the past quarter century, the interplay of experience and reflection, the rereading of Scripture and explorations into the history of Christian practice, have yielded some insights. As disciples of Jesus in a world of many religions, we strive to be *speakers of truth* who *pay attention* to those outside our usual assemblies; who seek out opportunities to be *hospitable* to all, including and especially people of other religions; and who learn to live in this religiously plural world as *good guests* and even as *pilgrims*. Perhaps it is just so that we can best bear witness to the love of Christ in this world— a world where we may live "not in fear of our neighbors," but in anticipation of learning, insight, friendship, and blessing.

In some ways, there is nothing new here. But just as "the old, old story of Jesus and his love" is heard anew in every telling, so Jesus' call to discipleship and to love the neighbor may be lived anew in every new day and the encounters it brings. For North American Lutherans in this time—and in the decades beyond—many of these encounters will be of the inter-religious kind.

FOR DISCUSSION

1. Look around your community/neighborhood. What religious groups are represented there? What places of worship do you find? Has the religious map of your community/neighborhood changed in the past years? (See www.pluralism.org/directory.)

2. Does your congregation, or individuals within it, have any relationships with these groups (mentioned in question 1) or their members? Share, if you are willing, about a friendship that you have with someone whose faith is different from your own. Has that friendship made a difference in how you understand your friend's religion and community?

3. Discuss the biblical "outsider" stories mentioned in the chapter. Can you think of others? Can you give examples from your own experience of times when it has been the "outsider" (to the familiar Christian community) who has brought "blessing, hospitality, practical help, or . . . a true word of rebuke"?

4. What does *hospitality* mean to you? Can you share a story about providing hospitality to others—even when that seemed hard? Or can you relate a story about receiving hospitality from others, in ways that moved you? Thinking about some of the religious groups in your own community/neighborhood (see question 1), what might inter-religious hospitality look like?

5a. Have you ever participated in something you would call a "pilgrimage"? What was it like? What personal investment did you put into it? Were you changed by it?

  b. Does the notion of pilgrimage "to one another as to a holy site" make any sense to you? In your community, what might that look like?

Yom Kippur Mutual Hospitality Between Jews and Christians: Northern California Lutherans Serve as *Shomrim* for Jews and Join in the "Break-Fast" Feast

Rev. Peg Schultz-Akerson, D.Min., a pastor of the Southwest California Synod (ELCA)

When hate crime vandalism occurred on Yom Kippur a number of years ago in the parking lot of a Sacramento area synagogue, Congregation Beth Israel of Chico, California, was saddened and also concerned that something similar could happen again, and to other synagogues. They responded by asking for the help of Faith Lutheran Church, also of Chico. Would we be willing to serve as *Shomrim* (guardians) for them while they observed Yom Kippur the following year?

The task was simple. Faith Lutheran volunteers would take turns standing watch in the parking areas around the temple throughout the High Holy Day observances while our Jewish neighbors were inside the temple in prayer. The Lutherans have been serving in this capacity ever since, never having a lack of volunteers for this neighborly care. A table spread with cookies, nuts, and fruit is provided by our Jewish friends even though they are fasting. During those days, hardly a worshipper walks by the *Shomrim* without expressing a gesture of heartfelt gratitude for our being there. The Christians who share in guarding the parking lot are also warmly invited to join our Jewish friends in the festive meal that breaks their fast at the end of Yom Kippur.

Friendships have developed over the years, and we are grateful that no harm has ever been done to the cars or campus of Congregation Beth Israel during these prayerful days. Faith Lutheran people are honored to have been asked to support our Jewish neighbors in this concrete act which becomes in turn an event of mutual hospitality as we celebrate together at the feast. Congregation Beth Israel's Rabbi Julie Hilton Danan sent a letter to Faith Lutheran expressing their gratitude, but more widely read was her expression of appreciation on her Facebook page. Good words travel fast.

As others and I have reflected on this experience, we have been struck by the creativity and trust on the part of Congregation Beth Israel as they looked at their own need. They wisely imagined looking outside themselves for help. While hesitancy may be common among us to ask for help beyond our usual support systems of family and close friends, those who risk asking for help more broadly may be giving a great gift in return. An insight drawn from this exchange between synagogue and church is that it was instigated by a request for help from the wider community.

This experience reminds me of the years my former congregation, St. Paul's Lutheran, Santa Monica, California, asked Jewish neighbors to cover our childcare needs on Sunday morning. The Santa Monica Synagogue worshipped on Friday evenings in our sanctuary, and they were pleased to respond to our need on Sunday mornings. The childcare provider also became a loving resource for teaching the children about other faiths even while they were very young: "Train children in the right way, and when old, they will not stray" (Proverbs 22:6, NRSV). My own children were often cared for in this Sunday morning nursery where they learned early on to cherish our Jewish neighbors, as they still do.

What if we were to open ourselves to asking for help more often outside our various groups? By asking for help we gift each other with experiences of giving that nurture and expand our own hearts even as we fulfill a neighbor's need. Service clearly benefits not only the served.

A Prayerful Place: Trinity Evangelical Lutheran Church in Wexford

Prepared by Kathryn Mary Lohre, based on an interview with former Pastor Frederick Schenker, November 24, 2014

About ten years ago, a group of Muslims had joined together to form an *ummah*, or worshipping community, in North Pittsburgh. While they were in the process of buying land and raising money to build a mosque, they approached several local churches to request use of their space for worship—including weekly Friday mid-day prayers and daily prayers during the month of Ramadan. Each time, they received the answer, "No." Without losing hope, the Muslims approached the pastor of Trinity Evangelical Lutheran Church in Wexford.

Pastor Schenker felt that this could be understood as part of the church's extended ministry to the larger community. (After all, secular groups used the building for their meetings.) But he also felt that extending hospitality to their Muslim neighbors was an appropriate response to Christ's calling: "Our Lord Jesus Christ said to love one another, don't judge, and if they're doing good things, support them."

A few years before, he had participated in the Abrahamic Initiative of the Chautauqua Institute and had learned about the value of understanding our differences and commonalities as "children of Abraham." He used this as a framework for the conversation he led with the church council to consider the Muslims' request. After a time of deliberation, a large majority of the church council was in agreement. Trinity Evangelical Lutheran Church invited the *ummah* into its parish (fellowship) hall. In turn, the *ummah* agreed to help the church with its needs, including clean-up days.

But of course things didn't end there. The first year the Muslims celebrated Ramadan at Trinity, they invited the Lutheran congregation to join them in breaking the fast. Over time, through such events, relationships developed along with friendships. For example, the wife and friends of Dr. Akbar, one of the Muslim leaders, joined Pastor Schenker's wife and her friends for a breakfast conversation about their respective faiths and a time of fellowship.

The Muslim community continues to build its Islamic Center, which when completed will include a prayer area, a multi-purpose hall for youth activities, meetings, classes and social events, and a fully-equipped kitchen. In the meantime, the extended families of Muslims in North Pittsburgh—people living in Egypt, Palestine, Afghanistan, Pakistan, and elsewhere around the world—have come to know Trinity Evangelical Lutheran Church as a place that, as part of its faithfulness to Christ, openly and unconditionally welcomes Muslims to pray. Pastor Schenker reflected, "I think that what we're doing here is going to be key for Christ's mission in the world in the twenty-first century."

CHAPTER TWO

Guidelines for Interacting in the Real World

Carol Schersten LaHurd

Introduction

One very good way to meet members of the ELCA and learn about their concerns is to travel around the country leading Bible study workshops. During much of 2014, I had the privilege of doing just that as author of the Women of the ELCA Bible study series for 2014-15, *Transforming Life and Faith*. Discussion in the workshops centered on themes like "Faith in the Family" and "Suffering and Endurance" and on Bible stories like David and Bathsheba and Paul's encounter with Lydia, a dealer in purple dyed goods. But often during the question periods, instead of asking me to elaborate on a biblical topic, the first woman to raise her hand would ask, "Please tell us what to think about Islam and Muslims." Throughout the yearlong study I had inserted illustrations from Judaism, Islam, and Buddhism, and apparently that approach had opened the door for serious questions about how people can be both faithful to their Christian commitments and welcoming to people of other religions. Considering the ways ethnic and religious ties appear to be intensifying violent conflict around the world, it is no surprise that Lutheran lay people and pastors are seeking answers and understanding.

This three-part chapter provides constructive models for inter-religious interaction by describing actual efforts in congregations and institutions. Dozens of case studies from people across the ELCA are organized into three groups:

- Part 1, Sharing Spiritual Life, including communal worship, fellowship, ministry and inter-religious families;

- Part 2, Sharing The Life of the Mind, including dialogue, shared scripture study, and joint resource production;
- Part 3, Sharing Practical Life and Service to the World, including dealing together with social issues like stereotypes and hate crimes; sharing physical space and resources; collaborative social action, advocacy, and service to the world; and non-congregational settings for interaction, such as hospitals, the military, and prisons.

Naturally, when I tried to make things clearer by dividing concrete real world experiences into three neat groups, I realized how much overlap there can be. For example, studying the story of Moses and the Exodus in the Bible and the Qur'an in a group of Jews, Christians, and Muslims is not only an exercise for our minds. As friendships develop and sacred scripture is explored, the study becomes spiritual and relational as well as intellectual. And such a study can lead to practical projects like joining together to build a Habitat for Humanity house. That said, I hope the three categories will guide our exploration of this broad question: How can we as Christians live and interact with our neighbors from other faith traditions? In addition, these unique and concrete stories can take us into the lives of people who are following Mark Swanson's models for engaging others in Chapter One—by speaking truth, attending to outsiders, practicing hospitality, and becoming pilgrims.

LEARNING FROM THE ROMAN CATHOLIC MODEL

Fifty years ago the Roman Catholic Church officially acknowledged the truth in other religious traditions and the value of inter-religious relations in the 1965 Vatican II document, *Nostra Aetate: Declaration on the Relation of the Church to Non-Christian Religions.* That bold step, along with similar streams of influence across worldwide Christianity, has led the way for interfaith initiatives by the ELCA and its predecessor church bodies. In 1991 the Vatican issued a new statement, *Dialogue and Proclamation: Reflection and Orientations On Inter-Religious Dialogue and the Proclamation of the Gospel of Jesus Christ* (issued jointly by the Pontifical Council for Inter-Religious Dialogue and the Congregation for the Evangelization of Peoples). The document's outline of the several forms of dialogue can guide our own exploration of the many ways Christians today are encountering inter-religious others:

1) The *dialogue of life*
2) The *dialogue of action*
3) The *dialogue of theological exchange*
4) The *dialogue of religious experience*

PART 1. SHARING SPIRITUAL LIFE
Gathering for Worship

Every summer in the Blue Ridge Mountains of North Carolina, the Greater Carolinas Rabbinical Association sponsors an Interfaith Institute for rabbis, their spouses, and invited Christian clergy and scholars. Each evening a different Christian tradition leads a vespers service; each morning a different strand of American Judaism conducts a brief Torah service. When the Lutherans lead vespers, many of the attendees who are practicing Jews may be hearing, for the first time, readings from the Gospels and hymns like "Beautiful Savior." At daily morning worship the Christians are privileged to hear forty rabbis reading the Torah aloud in Hebrew.

Those annual Jewish-Christian gatherings in North Carolina show one kind of interfaith worship: Each faith group worships in its own style, as if it were doing so without guests from other religious traditions. In another major type, people from various religions do their best both to be true to their own traditions and at the same time to be inclusive. In 1984, reports Pastor James Boline, "St. Paul's Lutheran Church in Santa Monica took a bold step and offered shelter to a fledging Jewish congregation, The Santa Monica Synagogue." One result of this invitation has been since 1985 an annual interfaith service on the Wednesday evening before Thanksgiving. The practice continued even after the synagogue moved to its own space and new clergy arrived in each congregation. Pastor Boline and his counterpart Rabbi Jeff Marx shared that although they as "clergy had already bonded with one another and were excited by the idea of an interfaith service. . . . This was a new experiment for the church, and some were a bit leery of sharing space with another group in a small structure." But

Santa Monica, California, Jewish and Lutheran clergy stand in front of a quilt depicting Jerusalem: Pastor Jim Boline, St. Paul's Lutheran Church; Rabbi Jeff Marx, The Santa Monica Synagogue; Pastor Peg Schultz-Akerson, Southwest California Synod.

both wanted to "send the sub-textual messages: 'look how well we—two different faith groups—share the same space' and, 'what a blessing it is to both offer and to receive hospitality and shelter.'"

The ways in which Pastor Boline, Rabbi Marx, and their congregations grew during these shared experiences demonstrate the value of an action-reflection approach to inter-religious learning. As they experimented with shared worship, they analyzed and reflected on the impact of including distinctively Jewish and Christian elements, as well as those held in common. Their intentional evaluation and reflection yielded new ways of interacting and new levels of mutual understanding.

Merging many different traditions into one celebration can be an even more challenging type of shared worship. A good example is the annual Interfaith Prayer Service to End World Hunger in Des Moines, Iowa, submitted for this project by Pastor Chris Olkiewicz, president of the Lutheran Ecumenical and Inter-Religious Representatives Network. Speaking at the October 2013 event were Cardinal Peter Turkson, president of the Pontifical Council for International Justice and Peace, and the Rev. David Beckman, president of Bread for the World and 2012 World Food Prize Laureate. Many religious leaders contributed worship elements: a hymn from Zambian Christians, prayers to end world hunger from the Jewish and Buddhist traditions, and a song from Sudanese women during the East African famine of the 1980s. Planning and implementing such an event is not as easy as we might think.

Cardinal Peter Turkson, president of the Pontifical Council for Justice and Peace, delivered the Newman Lecture at Drake University's Sheslow Auditorium. To his left is Des Moines Bishop Richard Pates and, right, Father Mark Owusu.

The event coordinator in 2013 was Kyle Lechtenberg, former diocesan director of worship for the Diocese of Des Moines and currently with Our Lady's Immaculate Heart Parish in Ankeny, Iowa. He says that this annual event requires the planners to be very clear and frank about what is acceptable and what is not—in order, as well as possible, to avoid comments by speakers that could be seen as offensive to some people from other religious traditions. Thoughtful diplomacy is important. One year an African immigrant Christian set up an altar cloth picturing Roman Catholic leaders. Lechtenberg gently reminded him that the church would be shared space and that something so obviously Chris-

The October 2013 interfaith prayer service to end world hunger was held at St. Ambrose Cathedral, Des Moines, Iowa. Photos by Mark Hommerding/Diocese of Des Moines.

tian should be cleared by the group beforehand. Eventually the leaders from Jewish and Muslim traditions approved leaving the cloth in place. But more than the outcome, it is the process of shared decision-making that demonstrates respect for the diverse sensibilities of the participating communities. Reflecting further, Lechtenberg says his reward for all the advance planning has been "seeing our cathedral filled with people of many faiths and being a house of prayer for all people."

The work of Christian leaders highlighted here shows that sharing worship across inter-religious boundaries can be both challenging and rewarding. Pastor Chris Olkiewicz suggests that the 350 people of diverse religious traditions who in Iowa annually pray together in response to world hunger make the biblical connection between "liturgy" (from the Greek *leitourgia*) as both worship and service. In California, Pastor James Boline understands the thirty-year tradition of Jewish-Christian Thanksgiving celebration as one that carefully honors the distinctiveness and commonalities of both traditions. In both Des Moines and Santa Monica, combining action with reflection has helped leaders develop effective ways of planning and worshiping together. In the process many people have learned about their differences and similarities in worship language and practice. But they have also become friends, able to share religious life.

Nurturing Fellowship

The population of Oak Lawn, Illinois, just south of Chicago, is now 15 percent Palestinian Muslim. The past few summers the Muslim and Christian communities have held a series of joint potluck suppers in a city park. They draw about 100 people to share ice breaker activities and main dishes donated by a local Arab restaurant. As is the case for sharing worship, sharing food across ethnic and religious lines requires sensitivity to differences. Ohio's Trinity Lutheran Seminary, as noted in Chapter One, hosts an annual Summer Seminary Sampler for high school students. In 2011 then-director Laura Book added the component of the first Youth Interfaith Dialogue for Columbus. Youth from mosques and synagogues joined the Christians for conversation and meals. In subsequent years vegetarian and kosher meals were added, and the Muslim fast for Ramadan had to be considered in scheduling the event one year.[1]

The annual Interfaith Seder Experience in Southern California now attracts several hundred people, so many that it is necessary to rent a large tent. Sponsored by the Claremont Interfaith Working Group for Mideast Peace, the event is not a formal seder (since that is a specifically Jewish religious observance), but rather a meal and program modeled on the Jewish Passover seder. Hosting the fellowship event rotates among the Jewish, Muslim, and Christian institutions—a feature that gives each group a chance to be hosts and to be guests. The March 2015 theme was "Our Journeys from Slavery to Freedom."

Claremont, California, mayor Cory Calaycay shares how significant the Interfaith Seder Experience is for building peace.

The same group also sponsors an annual September Interfaith Walk for Unity and Friendship that can draw up to 700 people, including many youth. The route makes stops at the worship spaces of various

---

1 For more ways ELCA seminaries are engaging religious others, see Case Studies 3: Campus Initiatives, "Seminary Interfaith Learning: Beyond the Books to Engagement," 115.

Rabbi Jonathan Kuputz and Cantor Paul Buch at Temple Beth Israel, a stop along the route of the annual Interfaith Walk for Unity and Friendship in Pomona, California.

Son William and father Don from Prince of Peace Lutheran Church, Covina, California, at the Annual Interfaith Walk for Unity and Friendship.

This emblem was used on T-shirts for the 2014 Interfaith Walk for Unity and Friendship.

religious traditions, such as a brief songfest at Temple Beth Israel in Pomona, a Reform synagogue that takes part in both annual interfaith events. One of the planning leaders is Pastor Thom Johnson, director of the Center for Lutheran Studies at Claremont School of Theology and pastor of Prince of Peace Lutheran Church. His assessment of the annual walk: "There is nothing like face to face encounter." Said another participant, "The people were radiant with joy . . . doing something positive to bring the community together at a local level that could have global implications."

A Muslim-sponsored program for meal fellowship is Abraham's Tent, an activity of the Niagara Foundation, with offices in several mid-western states. The idea is for diverse participants to gather in homes by neighborhood. The meal my husband and I hosted a few years ago included eleven attendees from the Jewish, Muslim, Roman Catholic, Methodist, and Lutheran traditions. Having lived twice in Arab Muslim countries, we were careful to provide vegetarian dishes along with meat entrees that met the requirements of halal, similar to kosher food rules for Jews. I had baked pumpkin pies for dessert. Only at the last minute did I bother to read the ingredient list on the ready-to-bake piecrust package. What an unpleasant surprise to see they in-

Peace walkers in Pomona, California, part of the Annual Interfaith Walk for Unity and Friendship.

cluded lard, a pork product not permitted for Jews and Muslims! Luckily we had an alternative dessert to serve. But the experience was a humbling reminder of the care and respect due inter-religious guests.

At first glance, enjoying each other's cuisines may seem a rather trivial way to interact across religious lines—until we remember the central importance of meal fellowship in Jesus' ministry. Offering and receiving the hospitality of food was a sign of respect, acceptance, and trust. The more we sit together at meals, the more we get to know others as human beings. Once we know them, we can see them more fully as the neighbors we are called to love and serve.

Serving Inter-Religious Families

The goal of authentic relationship across religious boundaries becomes a matter of necessity when families are inter-religious. Current research puts the "mixed" marriage rate in the United States at 42 to 45 percent, including marriages between Christians of different backgrounds, as well as between one who is religious and one who adheres to no religion. Therefore, Christians need to be sensitive to inter-religious family life within their own communities and for their neighbors of other faiths.

The ELCA and several of its ecumenical partners, along with the National Council of Churches, have identified inter-religious marriage and

BEGINNING TO ANSWER: "Why seek friendship with people of other religions?"

- Passages in both Testaments call us to love our neighbors as ourselves, even when those neighbors are strangers. To love our neighbors, it really helps to know our neighbors.

- As S. Mark Heim puts it in *Salvations: Truth and Difference in Religion* (1995), we need to know other religious traditions to better understand our own. In addition, we need both to honor what's distinctive about Christianity and respect the comparable aspects of others' faith traditions.

- Sharing food and hospitality across religious and ethnic boundaries can form communities of care and respect. Interviewing hundreds of diverse Americans, the authors of *Common Fire: Leading Lives of Community in a Complex World* discovered that "successive experiences over time create a way of being in the world which is continually open to rediscovering that 'we' and 'they' share common bonds."

- Through such transformative human contact, we can not only become better citizens of a multi-cultural America, we also can contribute to God's goal of shalom, peace and harmony for human community and for all of creation.

families as an area of growth—for learning, for ministry, and for resource development. Perhaps there is much to be learned from our Jewish partners, who have a strong track record in tending to this issue. The various branches of American Judaism respond differently on this issue. Some rabbis refuse to officiate at interfaith wedding ceremonies, as according to Jewish law, a Jewish marriage by definition is between two Jews. On the other hand, many Jewish congregations include non-Jewish spouses, partners, and children in their congregational lives. For Reform Jews, who are the ELCA's only bi-lateral Jewish dialogue partners, this is more the rule than the exception, to the point that there are often non-Jewish individuals on synagogue boards. The real interest in these communities is to try to integrate non-Jewish family members as much as possible so that, regardless of individual convictions and commitments, the family can also claim a Jewish identity. Often that identity can be nourished by study of related educational resources—many of which are available online. More recent developments within the diversity of American Islam also mirror this trend. Therefore, the resources of inter-religious partners could be instructive as Christians more fully explore this reality and develop further resources for inter-religious marriage and ministry with inter-religious families.

Finding or creating inter-religious wedding rites is a related challenge, and part of a larger need for inter-religious rituals. "Where can I find resources for conducting a Jewish-Lutheran memorial service?" was a Chicago pastor's first question at a meeting to introduce resources for congregational inter-religious awareness and education. He was referred to local groups and websites, organized informally by Jewish and Roman Catholic families. Lutherans, working with ecumenical partners, have an opportunity to do more to provide ministry with and ceremonies for inter-religious families. In contemporary America it is not only families who are multi-religious; increasing numbers of individuals identify themselves with more than one tradition. Some people may combine Reform Jewish practice with Zen meditation, or they may routinely attend both Muslim and Christian worship services. Many more see themselves as seekers of "multiple religious belonging."[2]

What have we learned so far about how people from differing faith traditions might share and enrich each other's lives spiritually? We have seen the benefits and challenges of shared worship experiences. We have discovered the value of starting with meal fellowship—to get to know the other much as Jesus did as he traveled Galilee teaching and preaching. Finally, we have considered the particular needs of families of mixed religious affiliations. In part 2, "Sharing the Life of the Mind," we encounter several ways inter-religious partners can enrich each other's lives theologically.

Planning to Share Worship and Fellowship

What have we learned?

- Planning for and sharing worship experiences can increase theological understanding and build friendships.

- Sharing meal fellowship can teach us about community life in various religious traditions and help build true cross-cultural and inter-religious friendships.

- To serve the increasing numbers of mixed-religion families, we can collaborate with ecumenical and interfaith partners to create spiritual and educational resources.

---

2 See, for example, *Many Mansions: Multiple Religious Belonging and Christian Identity*, ed. Catherine Cornille (Eugene, Oregon: Wipf & Stock, 2002), as well as material on the website of the Pluralism Project at pluralism.org.

- Approaches may differ with the particular inter-religious groups involved. An illustrative resource is the ELCA's 1998 "Guidelines for Lutheran-Jewish Relations," listed in the Appendix resources.

What should we be careful about?

- Become aware of the worship practices and theology unique to each tradition and plan how to educate participants about them.
- Consider including worship practices and theological perspectives held in common, such as respect for God's Ten Commandments in Judaism, Christianity, and Islam.
- Decide whose sacred space to use and/or plan to alternate among traditions.
- Take turns being both host and guest; be aware that many Christian churches are not used to giving up the control of being hosts.
- Decide whether and how to address "sticky issues," such as the divinity of Christ or Jews as God's chosen people or Muhammad as the "seal of the prophets."
- Plan to involve lay people, and a balance of women and men, for both hospitality and discussion of beliefs and practices.
- Brief participants about sensitivities before a meeting, such as the preference by some Muslims not to shake hands with unrelated persons of the opposite sex.
- Learn about dietary and calendar restrictions, such as observance of the Jewish Sabbath from sundown on Friday to sundown on Saturday.
- Be willing to take risks and accept responsibility for mistakes made along the way.

What might we try?

- Plan activities that bring people of different backgrounds together, even for activities not overtly religious, such as an interfaith book club that reads and discusses all type of books.
- Begin with fellowship events, such as a potluck picnic in a public park.
- Build friendships before planning shared worship, study, or dialogue.
- Organize an interfaith film night for all the major religious traditions in your community.

What should we be prepared for?

- Prepare for discomfort by some participants and allow them to voice their concerns and help them work through them without seeing them as failure.

- Take note of and celebrate increased mutual understanding and appreciation for other religious traditions within your own community.

- Help adult participants see that they are modeling for children and youth the value of respect and friendship.

FOR DISCUSSION

1. Choose one or two of the case studies demonstrating shared worship (such as the Jewish-Lutheran Thanksgiving service in Santa Monica) and discuss:

   - What surprised you about this story?

   - What troubled you, or prompted further questions?

   - What are some ways you might follow their example to create an interfaith worship experience in your own setting?

2. List quickly some types of fellowship events shown by the cases in this section. What factors made them successful? Discuss how you might craft an event with inter-religious neighbors.

3. Read together the sidebar, *Beginning to answer "Why seek friendship with people of other religions?"* Discuss particular statements with which your group members strongly agree and/or disagree.

4. Give the group members a minute or two to ponder ways in which their own families may be inter-religious and then share experiences in groups of two or three for five to ten minutes. Next report to the large group and discuss the questions: Where religious differences exist, how have they challenged family life? Enriched family life?

PART 2. SHARING THE LIFE OF THE MIND
Fellowship Leads to Dialogue

As North American church bodies began to reach out to other religious groups, the common model was inter-religious dialogue events and panels, usually organized by denominational staff and attended by clergy and professors. But at the grassroots level, new models are emerging. The catastrophic attacks of September 11, 2001, prompted many pastors and lay people to learn about other religions. One example is shared by Pastor Susan Strouse of First United Lutheran Church in San Francisco. Her experience highlights the promise and challenge of interfaith education at the grassroots. Just after 9/11, her congregation held a forum with a series of guests from Buddhism, Islam, Judaism, and Hinduism, in order to study these religions and to meet their neighbors of other faiths. After one session, Pastor Strouse reports, a participant told her "how much she was enjoying the study of Hinduism. But she was worried that if she accepted a Hindu's path as valid, she would be 'betraying Jesus.'" Strouse summarizes, "I reassured her that, given her firm foundation in Christianity, an exploration of other faiths would not endanger her soul." Reflecting on this incident, Strouse recognized that her parishioner had raised an important question for today's Christians. Much fuller discussion of this case and its implications are included in Chapter Three.

Whether or not their religious organizations are part of a formal inter-religious study series, as people share meals and life stories, they also begin to ask questions about each other's faith traditions. As mentioned earlier in this chapter, in Oak Lawn, Illinois, the summertime potluck suppers have led to a formal dialogue series with representatives from six Oak Lawn churches and the Bridgeview Mosque Foundation. A goldfish bowl format (with the discussion panel at a table and observers seated around them) allows for formal discussion among regular participants, followed by a question and answer session with all who attend. The planners began with down-to-earth topics such as "Food Rules: Formal and Informal." Congregations who are interested in starting their own inter-religious dialogues might try this approach, which can be less intimidating for all participants. Beginning with something familiar like Lenten and Ramadan fasting can lead to deeper theological discussions later. However, planners need to provide for additional information and explanations as questions arise: What are some reasons Muslims fast during the month of Ramadan? Why do many Protestant denominations no longer encourage fasting?

In the Atlanta area, Pastor Robb Harrell also discovered food as a step toward dialogue. He says that rapid growth in his suburban area has led to "an increasing number of encounters between people of different languages, races, nations of origin, and, most notably, different religions." Parishioners are asking him to help them understand the religious ideas they are encountering. When local Muslims gave a presentation on the basics of Islam during Ramadan one year, Harrell's wife cooked a Turk-ish fast-breaking meal or *iftar*. The guests shared their experiences as practicing Muslims in a post-9/11 United States. Then at sunset all shared both Turkish delicacies and more personal conversations. What can re-sult from this mix of food, fellowship, and dialogue? Says Harrell of the event with Muslims and similar encounters with Jews, Buddhists and Hindus: "What was most interesting to me was to see how the ground-work was laid for a future of trust and reconciliation. From the church's perspective, members were able to sit and meet with a person of anoth-er religion and learn from them in a way that was mutually respectful. Some questions were harder to deal with than others, but they were always asked and answered in a wonderfully respectful way. It helped us as Christians see past the social stereotypes we had of other religions that are perpetuated by media and the entertainment industry. No lon-ger were we talking about Buddhism or Islam in a detached manner. We were face to face with another human being, and that makes all the difference." Such experiences show that sharing a meal can develop the friendship and trust needed for theological conversation.

Congregations in college towns can sometimes more easily find inter-faith dialogue partners. First English Lutheran Church and Pastor Michael Short work with the students and staff at the University of Wisconsin–Platteville as part of their support for Lutheran Campus Ministries. At the "People of the Book, Faith" series, a few students from each of the three traditions—Judaism, Christianity, and Islam—lead discussions of faith practices. Their planning shows the value of agreeing first on ground rules: be respectful of others, show interest in learning about other faiths, work to dispel myths and misunderstandings. As the discussions moved to the difficult topic of factions within Christianity, local church leaders asked to participate, which Short says led to "a little more tension in the air as each wanted to make clear distinctions about what they believed." This raises an important question: Was the leaders' insistence on "clear distinctions" an obstacle to further dialogue or a valuable contribution? Some dialogue members may ask for more intense study of inter-religious differences as well as of common ground. This deeper level of dialogue requires careful study of each religious tradition—and a willingness by all participants to share their beliefs for mutual understanding rather than for judgmental comparison of religions.

A similar story comes from Michigan, where Pastor Fred Fritz has coordinated dialogue in this Michigan State (MSU) community through the congregation he serves. University Lutheran Church has joined with Sharey Zedek Synagogue, the Islamic Center of Greater Lansing, and the Red Cedar Neighborhood to sponsor two to three dialogue events each year. Each community hosts a meal and presentation on such topics as Judaism 101 and the ABCs of Islam. As part of the series, "Beyond Co-existence: Is It Possible?" a Muslim MSU professor shared the results of a Gallup poll showing that "only seven percent of all Muslims worldwide said they did not condemn the events of 9/11." People don't hesitate to raise hard questions in this university community. Christians ask Muslims to help them understand what motivates those Muslims who support or commit acts of violence. Muslims ask Christians to explain how they "justify a belief in the Trinity and the divinity of the Christ." And the participants recognize that authentic friendship and trust can make possible such challenging conversations.

Dialogue can also flourish in the congregational setting, especially when leadership is shared among the religious groups. Our Saviour's Lutheran Church in Arlington Heights, Illinois, hosted a six-part series on Islam and Christian-Muslim relations. Each Tuesday night more than a hundred people listened to a variety of Muslim and Christian speakers. Often as many as fifteen came from the nearby Rolling Meadows Mosque, which hosted the final event.

Regardless of the organizers' intentions for such congregational inter-religious dialogue events, there can be unpredictable outcomes. In the months following the 2011 tenth anniversary of 9/11, Ascension Lutheran Church in Cincinnati hosted a series open to the public. For one event a Muslim woman spoke about similarities and differences between Islam and Christianity, as well as common misconceptions of Islam. Pastor Joshua Miller was taken aback when some in the audience asked pointed, even hostile questions. Fortunately the speaker "did a marvelous job clearing up misperceptions and sharing her faith and a peaceful presence." When Ascension ended the series with a potluck supper, the fellowship hall was filled with Jews, Christians, Muslims, and interfaith families. Their lively conversation showed the worth of combining meal fellowship and informal inter-religious dialogue.

It is one thing to meet inter-religious others—and quite another to understand and love them. A series in San Luis Obispo, California, included talks by neighbors from Hinduism, Islam, Judaism, Roman Catholicism, and Protestant Christianity. Pastor Marjorie Funk-Pihl, at the time pastor of Mt. Carmel Lutheran Church, concludes, "We discovered that we share a similar vision: to live together with God in peace." The president of the local Islamic society adds, "If we maintain respectful interaction with each other and let people be, in a sense, then we can have a more peaceful relationship with each other, even if everyone just sticks to their own beliefs. Love thy neighbor doesn't mean agree with them. It means love them."[3]

Finally, it is important to recognize that inter-religious relations are not always easy, especially when there are strong disagreements within and among groups. Tensions can arise between Muslims and those from other religious groups on such points of disagreement as freedom of the press—when that freedom results in speech or cartoons blasphemous from an Islamic perspective. Some ELCA members know well how difficult conversations with our Jewish neighbors about the Israeli-Palestinian conflict can be. One important goal of authentic inter-religious friendship is to develop the ability to talk about troubling issues in an atmosphere of trust and respect. One success story in New York City is the Dialogue Project's Speaking Across Differences program, in which some local Lutherans participate. The Dialogue Project creates a safe environment for Christians, Muslims, and Jews from Israel and the Occupied Palestinian Territories to sit down with people from the rest of the world, such as Latino and Italian immigrants, to talk about topics like Israeli-Arab strife or combating homegrown terrorism. It is about

SOME INTER-RELIGIOUS DIALOGUE GROUND RULES

- The purpose is to learn, change, and grow, and to act on those new understandings.

- Such dialogue must be two-sided, within each community and between communities.

- Each person must be honest and sincere, and assume the same from the dialogue partners.

- Members must define themselves, and be able to recognize themselves in the other group's expressed portrayal of their tradition.

- People should come to the dialogue without strong assumptions about points of disagreement.

- Dialogue should happen between equals, e.g., not between Christian clergy and Hindu lay people.

- Participants must be willing to look critically at themselves and their own traditions.

- Each member should try to experience the other's religion "from within."

Adapted from "The Dialogue Decalogue" by Leonard Swidler, *Journal of Ecumenical Studies JES* rev 2003

3 www.thedialogueproject.org/SAD.html

having a safe place to have a difficult conversation. And it is about developing mature friendships across religious and ethnic boundaries.

The National Council of Churches' 1999 Policy Statement on Interfaith Relations and the Churches ends with six "Marks of Faithfulness." The fifth mark, "True relationship is rooted in accountability and respect," reads: "We approach others in humility, not arrogance. In our relationships we will call ourselves and our partners to a mutual accountability. We will invite each other to join in building a world of love and justice, but we will also challenge each other's unjust behavior. We can do both only from an attitude of mutual respect."[4] My own interfaith experience over the last thirty years suggests that such mutual accountability is no easy accomplishment. I have been part of several interfaith groups that have explicitly avoided any topics that might evoke serious disagreement, such as the Israeli-Palestinian conflict or divergent attitudes about religion and state. On one such occasion, forty Jewish, Christian, and Muslim scholars traveled to Skopje, Macedonia, to give leaders of that new republic advice about improving inter-ethnic and inter-religious relations. Yet, those same scholars could find no civil way to talk as a group about an issue important to many of them: how to work for peace in the Middle East. Even these academics trained in inter-religious relations had difficulty communicating with both honesty and respect. Perhaps they could have established ground rules for dialogue and given attention to building relationships and trust before opening up a difficult topic.

Reading Each Other's Scriptures

As conversations among people of different religious traditions become ongoing and trust deepens, participants are more likely both to acknowledge their differences and to talk about difficult issues. One of the most fruitful ways to reach that point is to read and discuss each other's sacred scriptures. In the late 1990s, a Lutheran pastor in Bethesda, Maryland, and a Conservative rabbi in Potomac established monthly discussions, often on books in the Torah, or what Christians call the Old Testament. How well have Jews and Lutherans come to know each other? Apparently they succeeded well enough that in 2011 Emmanuel Pastor Jan P. Lookingbill and Har Shalom Rabbi Leonard Cahan led a joint Holy Land trip. A second pilgrimage in 2012 visited the Spanish cit-

---

4 Full document at www.nationalcouncilofchurches.us/shared-ministry/interfaith/interfaithpolicy.php#mark.

ies where, during stretches of time in the Middle Ages, Jews, Christians, and Muslims found ways of living peaceably with one another.

In Bozeman, Montana, an ecumenical women's Bible study was held in a Methodist church and was led by a Lutheran, Pastor Jennifer Wilson, and a Jew, Rabbi Ed Stafman. One hundred people gathered in fall 2012 for large group lectures and small group discussions titled, "Windows into Genesis." The study was enriched by the rabbi's knowledge of Hebrew and the Jewish *midrash*, early commentaries on some of the Hebrew Scriptures that make up the Christian Old Testament.

College–congregation collaboration can create rich opportunities for interfaith scripture study. Augustana Lutheran Church in Chicago's Hyde Park neighborhood is the ELCA campus ministry site for the University of Chicago. Lutheran Campus Ministry and the Jewish Hillel program have sponsored lunch gatherings for Jewish and Christian students. Presentations and discussions have included such difficult topics as Martin Luther's legacy of anti-Judaism and study of Bible passages held in common. A series on "The Jewish Roots of Jesus" attracted members from the larger community, as Rabbi Niles Goldstein led a close reading of texts from the Hebrew Bible and the Christian New Testament. Lutheran Campus Pastor Elizabeth Palmer reflected, "What had begun within our ministry as a small group of Jewish and Lutheran students finding common ground on a campus that can be hostile toward faith has turned into a larger community that finds its faith enriched by gathering around questions of Jewish and Christian identity as people of the Book who are in this world together. We have also gained new insight into the person of Jesus: The fact that he was Jewish means that he didn't create a new religion, but rather he built on an existing one. And it helps us remember that he was human as well as divine (a fact that Christians sometimes tend to forget)." Two years later this Jewish-Lutheran friendship includes not only biblical and theological exploration, but also collaboration by Pastor Palmer and Rabbi Anna Levin Rosen on the University of Chicago's Sexual Assault Awareness Week, entitled "I Am My Sibling's Keeper." The plan is for religious leaders from a variety of faith traditions, including Islam, to share texts from their tradition that show cases of bystanders subtly intervening to prevent violence against another person, a plan that illustrates the potential for linking inter-religious dialogue and service to the world.

But shared scripture study can lead to unexpected obstacles, as well as new understandings. For example, understandings of revelation and sacred scripture vary among Jews, among Christians, and among Muslims. For most practicing Muslims, their holy book, the Qur'an, is seen as word-for-word the revelation of God to the Prophet Muhammad via the angel Gabriel and in the Arabic language. While some Christians have a similar view of the Bible's divine origins, many also see the Bible as conveying the Word of God in the words of human beings, in part influenced by their particular historical settings, and written in several languages over many centuries.

Thus, when two or more religious groups study scripture together, it is important to have leaders from each who can explain these different views of scripture and also similarities and differences for interpreting particular passages. A case in point is Abraham's near-sacrifice of his son, recorded in both the Bible (Genesis 22) and the Qur'an (Surah/chapter 37). Genesis clearly identifies the son as Isaac, Abraham's son with Sarah. Although the Qur'an does not name the son, Muslim readers over the centuries have believed him to be Ishmael (Ismail in the Qur'an), Abraham's son with Hagar, and the son viewed as continuing Abraham's lineage through Arabs broadly and through Muslims more narrowly. Reading these two stories side by side can reveal a great deal about the Judaism and Christianity of the Bible and the Islam of the Qur'an. But first one needs to consider how each story came to be—and how they came to have key differences, as well as similarities.

Producing Joint Resources

Sometimes inter-religious groups collaborate not only on theological dialogue and shared scripture study, but also on producing educational resources for broader use. As noted in this book's introduction, the ELCA's Consultative Panels on Lutheran-Jewish and Lutheran-Muslim Relations have each developed a series of "talking points" to explore difficult issues among the three Abrahamic faiths. The booklets, available for free download at the ELCA's Inter-Religious Relations website (www.elca.org/ecumenism), are suitable for youth and adult discussion of such topics as "Covenants Old and New," "Law and Gospel," and "Jesus and Mohammad in the Qur'an." Although Lutheran pastors and scholars were the primary authors, each resource was read by Jews and Muslims who offered corrections and additions. A much more intensive study of Jewish-Lutheran relations is contained the book, *Covenantal Conversations: Christians in Dialogue with Jews and Judaism*, and the accompanying DVD.

A very different collaboration is the *Discover Islam* DVD series, produced by Muslims in the United States and offered free of charge for use in ELCA churches and institutions. In order to make the series more useful for congregational education, a study guide was developed by the ELCA and A Center of Christian-Muslim Engagement for Peace and Justice (CCME) at the Lutheran School of Theology at Chicago (LSTC). Again, these are free downloadable resources, each matching one of the six DVDs on such topics as "Christianity and Islam" and "African-American Islam." Even though the study guide critically evaluates the series, the Muslim producers have welcomed the addition of the study guide, have made it available at the *Discover Islam* website, and have invited ELCA congregations and ecumenical partners to order sets of the DVDs.[5]

Yet another joint resource is "Standing Together," a video series and study guide produced by the Christian-Muslim Consultative Group of Southern California (formed in 2006), reports one of the project leaders, Pastor Thom Johnson, director of the Center for Lutheran Studies at Claremont School of Theology and pastor of Prince of Peace Lutheran Church in Covina. Both Muslims and Christians contributed to the videos and curriculum, which are intended to overcome stereotypes, to stimulate frank conversation about beliefs and practices, and to build relationships that might lead to future collaboration on efforts to benefit the larger community. Noteworthy is how the group shaped the resource. Everything in the study guide on Islam was written by Muslims, and everything on Christianity was written by Christians. This approach, perhaps more parallel than collaborative, ensured that each could present its own tradition.[6]

Part 1 of this chapter, Sharing Spiritual Life, outlined a number of ways congregations and other institutions can share worship and foster friendship and fellowship with people of different religious traditions. Part 2, Sharing the Life of the Mind, presented the challenges and benefits of shared study and dialogue. Part 3, Sharing Practical Life and Service to the World, will explore the many ways that individuals and groups can interact inter-religiously in practical life and in shared service projects.

---

5 DVDs at www.discoverislam.com/elca/; study guide at http://www.elca.org/Resources/ Ecumenical -and-Inter-Religious-Relations

6 See more at www.thecmcg.org/standing_together

Planning Shared Study and Dialogue

What have we learned?

- Successful inter-religious dialogue often begins with meal fellowship and conversation about the religious experience of members of the communities.

- Discussion of key differences and commonalities requires careful study and agreement on ground rules. [See "Some inter-religious ground rules" earlier in this chapter.]

- Shared scripture study can lead to much deeper understanding of our own Scriptures, such as how the Psalms picture God in comparison with the Qur'an.

- Inter-religious conversation can be difficult when there are strong disagreements within and among groups; this challenge can be addressed by building trusting, healthy relationships over time.

What should we be careful about?

- Work to include lay members and children and youth in inter-religious events. In some cases you may need to ask tactfully ahead of time about the other group's choice of participants, for example, whether Muslim women will be invited to be part of an inter-religious dialogue group.

- Find ways to give all participants a basic and objective introduction to the key beliefs and practices of other religious traditions, preferably before a shared event.

- Ensure that event leaders gain more in-depth knowledge of the other tradition, so that they can be aware of particular sensitivities, such as food restrictions, showing respect for the physical copy of the Qur'an, and handouts that might include God's name.

- Help participants understand the basics of their own tradition and prepare them to deal with differences in the other tradition that could be confusing or even disturbing to some.

- Take turns being host and guest as you move from fellowship to shared study and dialogue.

What might we try?

- Begin with meal fellowship in a neutral space, such as a park, and then move toward sharing each other's worship experiences and joint religious discussion and study.

- Start a dialogue group with very basic questions to help participants get to know each other and build trust. A series of meetings can focus on a topic for which each member will share, for example, "What is your earliest memory of encounter with God?"

- Schedule topics for discussion and have a person from each faith group prepare a short study: e.g., what do we believe about sacred scripture, the nature of God, prophets, God's mercy and compassion, ways of viewing ultimate reality without a transcendent deity.

- Allow time for practical matters, such as planning a shared meal or drafting a message to the media on an issue of concern.

- Let your study or dialogue group lead to additional shared activities, such as a joint community service project or a press conference after a destructive act of prejudice or hate in the local area.

- Invite seminary or college professors to lead, serve as resource people, and participate.

- Whenever you plan an educational event, such as talk by a local Buddhist monk, invite neighboring congregations to attend.

What should we be prepared for?

- Some participants may decide they are uncomfortable continuing in deep encounters with religious others; others may seek more such opportunities. However, even casual social encounters can be transformative.

- Participants may develop empathy for the other group that impels them to action and advocacy, such as speaking out against anti-Jewish remarks at work or unfair stereotyping of Muslims in a school setting.

- Some dialogue members may ask for more intense study of inter-religious differences as well as of common ground.

- Some participants will find their own beliefs and practices enriched by what they experience and learn from the other group: the value of memorizing scripture passages for use in prayer at set times each day as Muslims do, the importance of justice within the human community in Jewish understanding of God's law, or the value of mindfulness in everyday experience as practiced by Buddhists.

FOR DISCUSSION

1. This middle section of the chapter describes a number of inter-religious study and dialogue experiences. Discuss which ones you found most surprising and which your group might like to try.

2. Ask group members to recall times when they have felt challenged or threatened by the religious practices or beliefs of others. How have they dealt with such discomfort? What new approaches and resources have they found helpful so far in this chapter?

3. Review the material listed under "Planning Shared Study and Dialogue." In each sub-section ask participants to discuss the statements they find most helpful. Which potentially challenging issues would they like to explore further? As leader you may need to prepare to prompt discussion of particular issues.

4. If time permits, read the essay "Day of Dialogue: Neighbors in Conversation around Shared Interests" in Case Studies III to learn and discuss concrete ways to prepare for inter-religious conversations that can be both difficult and rewarding.

PART 3. SHARING PRACTICAL LIFE AND SERVICE TO THE WORLD

Dealing with Stereotypes and Hate Crimes

When bombs destroyed the Oklahoma City federal building in April 1995, many TV stations, newspapers, and American citizens immediately blamed Islamist extremists. At the time I was living in Minneapolis and helping to lead the Minnesota Muslim-Christian Dialogue. Within hours of the explosion I heard a sad story. The American-born woman who served as secretary at one of the local Islamic centers was driving to work when another motorist spotted her in the headscarf she wore as an observant convert to Islam. He followed close behind her car until she pulled into the center parking lot. He then rolled down the car window and yelled at her, "Go back where you came from!"[7]

As unwelcome and disconcerting as this encounter was, no physical harm came to the young woman involved. That was not the case for the Sikh gas station owner murdered in Arizona just four days after 9/11—or

---

7 For a creative approach to religious misunderstanding by an undergraduate student, see the essay by Caleb Arndt in Case Studies 4, 161.

for the six Sikhs killed by an avowed white supremacist in August 2012 at their temple in Oak Creek, Wisconsin. And of course such threats are not only aimed at Muslims or at people perceived to be Muslims. Think of the 2015 massacre of nine faithful black Christians studying the Bible at Mother Emanuel African Methodist Episcopal Church in Charleston, South Carolina. Many years ago in Sacramento, California, a synagogue parking lot was vandalized during the Jewish High Holy Day, Yom Kippur. The next year in Chico, California, Congregation Beth Israel feared a similar attack and asked for help from Faith Lutheran Church. Thus began a tradition of Lutherans serving as *Shomrim* (guardians) in the parking lot of their Jewish neighbors during Yom Kippur each year. Reports Peg Schultz-Akerson, pastor of Faith Lutheran Church, "Friendships have developed over the years and we are grateful that no harm has ever been done to the cars or campus of Congregation Beth Israel during these prayerful days."[8]

This church–synagogue story is noteworthy as an illustration of people's willingness to help others outside their own group. But, as Schultz-Akerson observes, the people of Beth Israel also showed "creativity and trust" when they risked asking for help beyond their "usual support systems." We can imagine a society where people who believe and worship differently routinely come together and care for one another with a sense of common humanity. And we can remind ourselves that care for the stranger is more than a nice thing to do. It is a central part of both Jewish and Christian ethics—and a biblical command.

Fortunately, even among the Americans who feel fear and hatred toward people of ethnic or religious backgrounds different from their own, only a few commit violent acts like synagogue vandalism or murder. But many others receive and pass on anti-Islamic or anti-Jewish email messages that then take on an appearance of truth as they multiply across the internet. Many such messages fail to distinguish between mainstream Islam and the violence-glorifying cults that pervert the Qur'an and Islamic tradition—or to acknowledge the violence perpetrated by many religious groups (including Christianity!) in regional conflicts.

What can be done about stereotyping of and bearing false witness against religious others? In the United States, the Shoulder to Shoulder Campaign consists of dozens of faith-based, inter-religious and religious organizations working to end anti-Muslim sentiment through both

8 Read more details about this unique relationship in the full case study by Pastor Shultz-Akerson in Case Studies 1, 43.

grassroots awareness-raising and advocacy. The ELCA and many other Christian bodies and leaders are fully engaged in this effort, and ELCA bishops have published op-eds clarifying the differences between mainstream Islam and the distortion of Islam cited by those who advocate violence or discrimination to advance their political goals. To prepare for future partnership and dialogue with American Muslims, the Shoulder to Shoulder Campaign also sponsors an Emerging Religious Leaders Seminar in conjunction with the annual Islamic Society of North America (ISNA) convention, attended by Lutheran and other Protestant seminarians.

In addition, faculty and chaplains from ELCA colleges and universities have been meeting with churchwide staff to strengthen interfaith engagement on campuses and to develop a network to encourage such engagement across various ELCA expressions.[9] This builds on prior work such as the "Facts, Faith, and Film-making" resource for reflection and discussion of portrayals of Jesus' Passion. Mel Gibson's 2004 film prompted this resource, which is useful for addressing the broader issue of stereotyping in the motion picture industry. Leading this effort and linking to the resource on its website is the Institute for Jewish-Christian Understanding, based at Muhlenberg, a college of the ELCA.

Even as we applaud these efforts to educate, we need to remember that it is not easy to overcome hatred and suspicion based on fear. In *On Immunity*, Eula Biss refers to the work of Paul Slovic on *The Perception of Risk* when she says, "Our fears are informed by history and economics, by social power and stigma, by myths and nightmares. And as with other strongly held beliefs, our fears are dear to us. When we encounter information that contradicts our beliefs, as Slovic found in one of his studies, we tend to doubt the information, not ourselves."[10]

In the face of such fear, it is good that diverse groups are working together to dispel prejudice on a national scale. The arts have become an increasingly effective way to confront stereotyping and unite communities. In Chicago, annual Sounds of Faith concerts celebrate ancient and modern music from the three Abrahamic faiths of Judaism, Christianity, and Islam. Each November the Lutheran School of Theology at Chica-

---

9   See, in Case Studies 3 and 4, examples from Augustana and Concordia Colleges and California Lutheran University.

10 *On Immunity: An Inoculation*, Graywolf Press Kindle Edition, locations 425-28.

go invites its Jewish neighbors to take part in a service of remembrance of Kristallnacht, the night when glass windows were broken as part of anti-Jewish violence around Germany in November 1938. Chicago's Silk Road Rising, housed in a downtown Methodist church, does both live theater and online videos that look at personal and political issues through primarily Asian-American and Middle Eastern-American lenses. Sometimes religious communities send small groups to attend and discuss the plays. During 2015, using the internet to collaborate with its potential audience, Silk Road Rising created a new play called *Mosque Alert*, the story of two suburban American families—one Christian, one Muslim—whose lives are disrupted by a proposal to build a mosque in their community.

Sharing Space and Resources

When the ELCA Consultative Panels on Lutheran-Jewish and Lutheran-Muslim Relations invited people from across the church to submit inter-religious case studies, some of the first stories we got were from churches that share space with mosques and synagogues. Years before they became formally involved in inter-religious dialogue, Pastor Michael Short's Platteville, Wisconsin, congregation gave local Muslims the use of their kitchen and fellowship hall for celebration of major Muslim feast days. Later when the same Muslims needed a new space for Friday prayers, says Short, "We again opened our doors."

Sometimes worshipping in each other's buildings requires creative solutions. Napa Valley Lutheran Church and Congregation Beth Shalom had been neighbors for many years. In fact members of Beth Shalom used to joke that they would tell visitors to "turn at the blue cross," a neon-blue image on the church's cinder-block tower. Sadly, that tower was lost in the August 2014 earthquake. But the church did host Congregation Beth Shalom during their 2013-14 synagogue renovation. The challenge then was what to do about another cross, the one in their sanctuary, during Jewish services. The answer was to commission a six-foot banner painted with a tree of life image to hang in front of the sanctuary's wooden cross. When Congregation Beth Shalom moved into their new building in fall 2014, they invited Napa Valley Lutheran Church to a special Friday night Shabbat service and a celebratory meal. Comments by Napa Valley's Associate Pastor Julie Webb demonstrate the educational value of such hospitality and collaboration: "I learned how deeply rooted our Christian practices and messages are in our parent faith of Judaism.

The vibrant and colorful *Tree of Life* banner used by Congregation Beth Shalom was created by artist Nina Bonos. Her *Joyous Judaica* images explore traditional and modern Jewish themes and symbols. Her art adds distinction to synagogues and other Jewish gathering places, professional office spaces, and residences across the U.S. and beyond.

Tree of Life 2 © Nina Bonos, 2015 www.ninabonos.com
Reprinted by permission of the artist.

Although I knew it before, I was struck by the similarities of their *bimah* [speaker's platform] to our chancel and altar, as well as of their messages of repentance at Yom Kippur to ours for Ash Wednesday."

Religious Neighbors Together—and Serving the World

In many cases interfaith friendships arise not in formal dialogues, but in efforts to meet concrete needs in local communities. Christians in DuPage County, Illinois, reached out to immigrant neighbors by sponsoring English language classes. Local Muslims got involved, and friendships developed. When the county zoning commission denied permission to construct a new mosque, Faith Lutheran Church in Glen Ellyn helped reverse the decision. Later Faith's pastor, Jim Honig, was keynote speaker at the groundbreaking for the new mosque. English as a Second Language classes also brought together Lutherans and Muslims in Indianapolis, as recounted by Pastor Bonnie Sparks and summarized in Chapter Three. Pastor Jane Buckley-Farlee reports that Trinity Lutheran Church in Minneapolis provides numerous services and activities for their African immigrant neighbors. Safe Place: Homework Help, a drop-in tutoring program during the school year, serves 120 school-age children, tutored by students from Augsburg College and the University of Minnesota. Trinity serves a community meal every Wednesday evening, and Trinity's parish nurse provides healing care twice a month in a neighborhood health initiative called "Health Commons." And the church hosted a local neighborhood Muslim community after their mosque was damaged by fire.

Do such efforts make a difference? Buckley-Farlee gives her answer: "Being a Christian presence in such a diverse setting opens the way for Trinity to continue bringing in God's Kingdom right in our midst in ways that we would never have expected, but are nonetheless real. And in that process we are changed. All of us." But serving an ethnically and religiously diverse local neighborhood is not always easy. Says Buckley-Farlee, "Being a Christian presence means letting go of any expectations and dreams of solving problems and fixing everything. It means letting the community lead and listening for ways we might, just might, be able to help. It means quietly realizing that being present and listening may be the real help that we can give this community." This very perceptive observation by Pastor Buckley-Farlee is a powerful reminder for all of us in our own lives. We often want to find ways to help others immediately—and seldom think that simply being there is a value. My husband and I have wondered about this with the refugees our Chicago congregation sponsors each year. When we do visit them, it is often to deliver something and hear them tell us what more they need. That fosters a dependency relationship. With our own friends and family, we often are just present for meals and conversation—but also supplying help whenever needed. We can follow Buckley-Farlee's lead and practice being present for our interfaith neighbors.

Beyond local communities and congregations, multi-faith groups are organizing around issues for both service and advocacy. Pennsylvania Interfaith Power & Light is one of many such state-wide organizations addressing issues of conservation and renewable energy. The Pennsylvania group consists of forty religious institutions working to reduce dependence on fossil fuels.[11] In Columbus, the B.R.E.A.D. Organization (Building Responsibility, Equality and Dignity) brings together many diverse Jewish and Christian congregations for such outreach as ensuring that non-violent juveniles are being dealt with not in the court system, but in "community based Restorative Justice Circles where they are held accountable for their actions and rebuild relationships within their neighborhoods."[12]

Nationally the ELCA's Washington advocacy office collaborates with many religious and secular nonprofit groups to address the needs of

---

11   Read more in Jonathan Brockopp's report in Case Studies 2, 85.

12   www.breadcolumbus.com

low-income and other vulnerable populations and to maintain just levels of American humanitarian aid, for example, in times of famine in Africa. A key partner is the Religious Action Center (RAC) of Reform Judaism. As far back as the 1970s ELCA staff worked with the RAC on ending wars in Central America, as well as on such domestic services as food stamps and WIC, the nutrition program for women, infants, and children.

Interfaith Interaction in Hospitals, Military Service, and Prisons

Spending time in a hospital with a family member undergoing serious illness and even death can be a very difficult and exhausting experience. Imagine what it might be like for Muslim immigrants watching their father approach his last breaths without any spiritual support or practical advice about American burial options. The Chicago-area Advocate Health Care System is one of many hospitals around the U.S. responding to the needs of increasing numbers of patients from many national and religious backgrounds. ELCA pastor Fred Rajan is vice president, Office for Mission and Spiritual Care, at Advocate Good Shepherd Hospital in Barrington, Illinois. He describes a few of the Advocate system's educational efforts: emails to staff announcing all major religious holy days, special training for chaplaincy staff on Muslim and Jewish traditions and beliefs, and "Lunch and Learn" presentations to introduce staff to various religions. Advocate Good Shepherd Hospital is actively involved in planning and leading the community-wide Interfaith Martin Luther King, Jr. Prayer Breakfast in Crystal Lake, Illinois. This event, planned collaboratively by Buddhists, Christians, Jews, and Muslims, draws 250 annually.

Rajan is understandably proud of "Heart to Heart," a hospital-organized volunteer group of Muslim lay people, both men and women, who make daily visits to Muslim patients and are on call for emergencies. He tells the story of a Muslim patient who died in the emergency room after many attempts to save her. Her family spoke little English and had gone home by the time the Muslim volunteers arrived. The two volunteers went to the family home and brought them back to the hospital for Muslim prayers and rituals. Next they found the family a funeral home with expertise in Islamic burial practices, and they cared for the family for several more weeks. Eventually these two volunteers received the hospital's Mission, Values, and Philosophy Award at a ceremony attended by a hundred hospital personnel.

To expand sensitivities toward Muslim patients throughout the Chicago area, the Lutheran School of Theology at Chicago (LSTC) works with local Muslim organizations to provide two-day chaplaincy workshops for spiritual care of Muslim patients. Besides an introduction to Islam, the seminar includes culturally and religiously sensitive concerns, funeral arrangements, grief and the afterlife, and such end-of-life issues as removing life support and organ donation. How can more of us support such efforts? We can ask our pastors and congregations to investigate how local clinics and hospitals are making their staff members sensitive to the needs of religiously diverse patient populations. And we can share these examples from the health care field to show how Lutherans are taking leadership roles in creating a civil society that welcomes and serves many types of American people.

The American military is another arena where ELCA members are serving multi-religious communities along with multi-religious colleagues. The Rev. Eric Wester, assistant to the presiding bishop and director of federal chaplaincy ministries for the ELCA, notes that ELCA military chaplains work closely with those representing the Protestant, Catholic, Jewish, Muslim, and Buddhist traditions. Wester explains that, while not all denominations are comfortable with having chaplains reach out beyond their own adherents, "military leadership applauds such efforts." He adds, "Chaplains seek out interaction as a way of developing better understanding of missions, religious groups in an area of operation, and learning better ways to work as an international team. This includes mutually working with religious freedom and its many different expressions by different faith groups, nations, and conflicts." One such chaplain is Scottie Lloyd, now a pastor in San Bernardino, California. Lloyd has also served as the ELCA Army Chaplain to the Third Army in Atlanta. During that service he was assigned to develop new relationships with religious leaders in a twenty-seven-country area of the world. In Jordan, for example, his efforts alleviated distrust and built friendship and collaboration among American Christian and Jordanian Muslim military chaplains.[13]

We may be surprised to learn of the efforts to develop inter-religious sensitivity and relationship in hospital and military settings. Perhaps even more unexpected is what's happening in some United States prisons. North Carolina has an Interfaith Prison Ministry for Women with the mission "to build bridges of hope for women in prison both before and after their release." In Ohio, men in three correctional facilities participate in the multi-faith Horizon Prison Initiative, spending a year living in a small

---

14 Read Pastor Lloyd's full account in Case Studies 2, 82.

dorm, studying together, and hearing representatives from diverse faiths. The benefits are enormous. Ohio spends $26,000 per inmate per year. Horizon costs only $1,600 per year and over ten years has led to a recidivism rate one-fifth that of the general prison population.

The story of retired ELCA pastor Bob Hanson further demonstrates the mutual transformation that can occur when people of diverse religions interact in meaningful ways. Bob and his wife, Karen, are deeply imbedded in the Lutheran tradition and have been enriched by serving in urban ministry. "Yet," says Hanson, "it is the walking on the path of the other that fills our lives with grace, understanding, and peace." For twelve years he taught English in Japan and served as a Navy chaplain and reservist for twelve more. Hanson, while remaining a Lutheran, also has been using some Zen Buddhist practices since the early 1990s. This background enables him to make twice-monthly visits to four state prisons for two hours of "spiritual practice, good conversation, and some quiet time" with prison Buddhist *sanghas* (assemblies or communities) that meet under the direction of the Milwaukee Zen Center. Hanson describes the results: "In the many years I have been serving these men in prisons, I have seen human beings turn their attitudes and lives around. Some of the most dramatic examples are the men who will never be leaving the prisons."

Tonen O'Connor is one of the Buddhist priests with whom Hanson serves in this prison ministry. One day as they were leaving a prison, Hanson told her how much he liked the men they work with. She replied, "Bob, these men are some of my best friends." Hanson concludes, "Yes, they are in prisons. Yes, they did something very unskillful to get there. Yes, they know it, and never a day goes by that they do not remember. But they are human beings, spiritual practitioners, men who want more than incarceration for their lives. In the case of these men, in these groups, it is the practice of meditation and the teachings of the Buddha. There is a thread that sews its way through all humanity; we need not fear the other, but embrace it and our neighbor's faith."

Moving Toward God's Shalom

Whether the setting for inter-religious engagement is a college, the military, a hospital, a prison, or a congregation, the particular cases described in this chapter illustrate the crucial importance of how we as Christians and as citizens engage people and groups who are different from us. When we vote and advocate political action, and when we inter-act in the workplace and in our neighborhoods, we need to think about what is good for everyone, not just for our own faith communities. The chief goal of this chapter is to spark new ideas and to provide insights and guidelines for engaging cultural and religious others in ways that both build up the larger society and strengthen our Christian commitments. A model for all of us is Lutheran Leymah Gbowee, one of three female recipients of the 2011 Nobel Peace Prize. This Lutheran-raised and Mennonite-trained leader used the power of friendships among the Muslim and Christian women of Liberia to end the Liberian civil war. Such inter-religious efforts may sometimes fail, but they are among the best ways to serve God's will for shalom for the human community and for all of creation.

Working Together on Real World Issues

What have we learned?

- Times of national and local crisis can both increase tensions among faith groups and create opportunities for constructive collective responses.
- Offering hospitality and use of physical space across religious boundaries can have positive ripple effects.
- Serving the needs of our neighbors regardless of their religion can help us develop inter-religious friendships and understanding.
- Hospitals, prisons, and the military offer unique opportunities for inter-religious engagement.
- Overcoming fear and stereotyping can have widespread benefits in civil society, as well as among religious groups.

What should we be careful about?

- Be aware that whenever particular groups feel threatened by vicious Internet messages, they are less likely to welcome inter-religious encounters, and they may need reassurance of our good intentions in seeking friendships.
- Take advantage of opportunities for building deeper relationships, for example, when religious groups share a physical facility or collaborate on a social service project.
- Listen carefully to underrepresented groups in your own community so that you can help develop programs for unmet needs, such as a clothing bank or English language classes.

- Recognize that many active church members are uninformed about the challenges those of other faiths deal with daily in such public institutions as schools, hospitals, and prisons.

What might we try?

- Use interfaith dialogue groups as a starting point for joint action on social problems, such as teenage drug abuse.
- Encourage interfaith leaders to form a "rapid response network," to assist communities affected by hate crimes and to correct media stereotyping of particular groups.
- Arrange for media coverage of successful inter-religious activities so that many more people will be aware of the benefits. (Or blog about it yourself!)
- Look for and join local programs that serve the spiritual needs of military personnel and prison inmates.
- Find out how local hospitals are sensitizing staff to caring for patients from many backgrounds.
- Encourage inter-religious understanding through shared experiential learning, such as building a house for Habitat for Humanity or attending a play about inter-religious issues.
- Volunteer to help settle a refugee family, as often those granted asylum come from varied religious backgrounds.

What should we be prepared for?

- The modeling of respectful relationships among diverse religious communities can be a catalyst for understanding and harmony in the larger society.
- Collaborations on social outreach projects can be productively unsettling, as they expose us to new problems to be faced, such as schools and employers that do not recognize the desire by non-Christians to attend worship and participate in major feast days.
- As Lutherans, we find ways to more fully live into our freedom in Christ to love and serve our neighbor.

FOR DISCUSSION

1. Reread the story from Pastor Jane Buckley-Farlee, whose congregation helps care for the Somali immigrants in their part of Minneapolis. Discuss her reflection that "being a Christian presence means letting go of any expectations and dreams of solving problems and fixing everything. It means letting the community lead and listening for ways we might, just might, be able to help. It means quietly realizing that being present and listening may be the real help that we can give this community." How might we apply this wisdom concretely in our local settings?

2. Give participants a few minutes to think about the following and then have a group discussion:

   • Which case studies in this section of the chapter most surprised you and why?

   • Which ones reminded you of your own experience?

   • Which inter-religious service projects would you like to try and why?

3. Discuss ways your own congregation or group might partner with religious others to minister to those in the military, in hospitals and/or in prisons.

Another Way to Peace

Pastor Scottie R. Lloyd, Chaplain (Colonel-Retired), United States Army, The Lutheran Church of Our Savior, San Bernardino, California

The 9/11 wars in Iraq and Afghanistan are fading. The current hotspots remain heated, but large-scale warfare is significantly reduced. Yet during these challenges a little-known peace effort occurred and continues today all over the world.

It started with a blank piece of paper, a vision of what could be, and a strong desire to foster peace as a preventive effort to conflict. My assignment as an ELCA Army Chaplain to the Third Army in Atlanta was to develop new relationships with religious leaders in a twenty-seven-country area of the world. The Army chaplaincy had never intentionally tried to accomplish this sort of mission on such a large scale before. The beginnings were daunting but doable with numerous singular successful events on record by other chaplains and sizable resources made available for support to such peaceful efforts.

After much research, thought, and prayer, Jordan was selected. Jordan's military has a well-established chaplaincy. It's modeled after the British Army, but there the resemblance fades. No one was quite sure how it was structured or how it reached out with religious support. Initial invitations were stalled, but after prayer and patience we

American Chaplaincy items on display: Christian, Jewish, Muslim, Buddhist. The fact that Americans try to provide religious support equally to all faiths has opened the door to a second round of talks and has begun establishing trust.

Gift giving after an inter-religious chaplaincy visit. Here the mufti presents a gift showing Petra, a site visited during this trip, to Chaplain (colonel) Adams-Thompson with Chaplain (Major) Abdullah Hulwe translating in the background. In 2015 Abdullah was one of only six Muslim imams in the United States Army.

finally received permission to send a team of four American Army chaplains and one chaplain assistant to Amman, Jordan. There we would introduce ourselves to our counterparts and share how we do religious support to soldiers and their families. They would reciprocate.

The team consisted of me, our supervisory chaplain, a senior sergeant chaplain assistant, an Army Muslim chaplain, and a Colorado National Guard chaplain. The National Guard chaplain was a participant in what the federal government calls the State Partnership Program. The Muslim chaplain, junior in service years, but a lifelong Muslim and fluent Arabic speaker/translator, provided invaluable assets to our well-rounded group.

Despite Arabic translation challenges for our team, diplomatic awkwardness for both chaplaincies, and suspicion from our hosts about why we Americans were visiting, this first foray of five days ended with warm feelings. Indeed, our hosts began to realize that we were really religious leaders and not cloaked CIA agents or publicity hounds for American causes. We really wanted to be friends, learn more about Islam from original sources closer to Mecca and Medina, and discover ways to promote peace in a volatile region of the world.

Another trip to Amman followed, cultivating deeper understanding. Both sides benefited in different ways, but always accomplishing the same end: a peaceful way to exchange truth and understanding that influenced how each side might approach dangerous issues in the Middle East from a faith-based perspective. Finally, we American chaplains arranged to host our new friends in the United States. Their Chief of Chaplains, or Mufti, came with a retinue of outstanding Jordanian chaplains whom we now knew and with whom we were on a first name basis.

What amazed our guests was pluralism in action both in our military ranks and in American society. They enjoyed a tour of Atlanta's newest mosque and conversed with fellow imams. They listened carefully to the briefings and enjoyed the foreign food. Our personal and professional sharing reached deeper levels especially as they met our families for the first time.

On the last day of their visit, protocol called for a formal exchange of speeches and gifts. Preceding this presentation was devotion. Each day began with devotion. I was scheduled to share on the last day. The day prior one of my Jordanian chaplain friends privately asked me why the American chaplains were sharing only from our Old Testament Scriptures during devotions. Why not share from the New Testament? "They want to respect your feelings about where we disagree on the person of Isa (Jesus)," I said. My friend frowned. "Be who you are as we have been," he offered. "This is how true friends are with each other." I smiled and related my text as the Beatitudes from Jesus. He smiled in return. Despite some looks from my American colleagues the next day, our Jordanian guests were moved hearing the Beatitudes and my confession of faith. A valuable lesson was learned by all: Be respectful. Be who you are, and allow the same from others.

Lastly, the Mufti rose and spoke through an interpreter. "When we were first approached with this exchange, we were not for it," he candidly shared. "You are infidels. Why would you want to see us? We wondered what you wanted from us. But we have seen the truth with our own eyes and heard with our own ears and have experienced it in new friendships with you." He explained that we genuinely care equally for all people—Christian, Muslim, and others alike. "There are voices that say you are a godless people who care only for yourselves," he continued. "These voices are wrong. You are people of faith. You could try and tell our people what you have shared with us, but they will not listen to you. You are still infidels. Our people will listen to us though. We are their religious leaders and are trusted. We will tell them the truth. We will share with them what we have witnessed. We will help still these violent voices with the truth." Tears welled in my eyes at this conclusion and later, when the Mufti and I shared a parting farewell, those tears returned.

This exchange is replicated all over the world now at strategic, operational, and tactical levels within our military chaplaincies. It's not an Army thing, but as it's always been, a multi-service inter-agency effort to prevent conflict with peace based on truth through personal relationships mutually beneficial to all parties. It's one way an ELCA chaplain-pastor, working for God and country, engaged people of other religions. It is the church at work in a different way through its chaplains. It continues to make a difference in a dangerous world today.

People of Faith Responding to Climate Change
Jonathan Brockopp, Grace Lutheran Church, State College, Pennsylvania

Inter-religious work is sometimes born out of necessity. I am deeply concerned about climate change, and that concern arises directly from my faith commitments. But frankly, there aren't a lot of Lutherans in my area of central Pennsylvania who feel the same way. Instead, I have found common ground with people of other faiths who are as concerned about this issue as I am. Together, we founded a Pennsylvania chapter of Interfaith Power & Light (PA IPL), a religious response to climate change. As people come to realize the importance of a faith voice on this issue, more are joining us, even members of my own congregation.

By design, the PA IPL board has representatives from different faiths (i.e., Judaism and Baha'ism) and several different Christian denominations. We all find strength and inspiration from working with folks from other traditions and learning how their faiths motivate them to act on climate. For some, it's a deep concern about justice—both for those suffering now from our changing climate and also for future generations. For others, it's a conviction that the earth itself is sacred and that we have a duty to protect it and all living creatures.

Pastor Steve Lynn preparing to bless the cyclists in 2013 (with Grace Lutheran Church members Cricket Hunter, director of programs and outreach for PA IPL, and Laurel Saunders, Grace Pre-school director).

PA IPL also finds common ground in helping congregations to save money on their energy bills. We find that synagogues and mosques are just like churches: The buildings are expensive and budgets are tight. By promoting energy efficiency, we help budgets go further. For example, looking around our church and preschool, we discovered that we had twenty-two individual refrigerators in the building! With a little discussion, we cut that number in half.

This is great work, but I wanted to do more, so in 2012 I organized a bicycle trip to Washington, D.C. The 200-mile trip took us five days, sleeping in church basements and people's homes, but we made it! When we arrived, we visited members of the Pennsylvania congressional delegation to urge action on climate change.

2015 bikers, including Grace Lutheran Church members Jon Brockopp, Molly Hunger, and Noah Droege, arrive in Washington, D.C.

Bikers on the 2014 trip receiving hospitality from Rabbi Fred Scherliner-Dobb, at Congregation Adat Shalom in Bethesda, Maryland. Also, shown, Grace Lutheran Church members Molly Hunter and Jason Whitney.

That first year it was three of us, last year twelve went on the trip, and already eighteen folks have expressed interest in joining the 2016 trip. Every year it gets better, with amazing people riding and hosting us. For example, we make a stop along the way at Congregation Adat Shalom, a Reconstructionist Jewish congregation that has worked hard to make its synagogue energy efficient; they even have solar panels on the roof.

Returning home to my congregation, Grace Lutheran Church in State College, I feel inspired to help our congregation develop a plan to significantly reduce our carbon emissions. After all, we go through an enormous amount of electricity every year, most of which is produced by coal-fired plants. If we could put solar panels on our roof, we could make a big difference.

Working with people of faith from across the state, I don't feel quite so alone. Sure, I wish I could point to more Lutherans leading the way on this issue, but I am grateful to my brothers and sisters from many faiths who are working now to leave a more beautiful world, one full of the diversity of God's handiwork, for our children.

CHAPTER THREE

Exploring the Uncomfortable Questions

THE EXPERIENCE OF INTER-RELIGIOUS WORK

Jonathan E. Brockopp

What initially attracted me toward this project were the compelling stories from congregations all over the ELCA that we received from our call for case studies. As a historian of religions, I know that stories are the most powerful means by which religious traditions communicate truth to their adherents, and so I wanted to write a chapter that captured some of the excitement of the inter-religious experience. Therefore, I include long excerpts from some of these cases, only lightly edited to convey the voices of their authors. As I was putting this essay together, however, I realized that there was a tension in these stories between those who felt that inter-religious encounters were positive and those who were worried about their negative consequences. Although I am strongly in favor of inter-religious work, I recognize the legitimacy of these important concerns. I hope that facing the uncomfortable questions head-on will encourage folks to take the risk and join the many ELCA congregations that have found these engagements to be an enriching experience.

On August 5, 2012, a lone gunman attacked a Sikh *gurdwara* (place of worship) outside of Milwaukee, Wisconsin, killing six before taking his own life. This terrible crime reverberated throughout the entire religious community in the area and beyond. Of course, Sikhs were devastated by the loss of their members and by the shooting of a renowned priest, Punjab Singh, who at last report is still immobilized from the attack. Tragedies like this are disturbingly common in our world, and while it is our Christian duty to show mercy and advocate for justice, it is hard to know what to do.

In Milwaukee, Christ Our Savior Lutheran church chose a unique path, inviting members of the *gurdwara* to join them in packing food supplies to be sent to Haiti. This may seem like an odd response, but not only has Christ Our Savior been packing food supplies to be sent to the hungry for years, Sikhs also engage in a sort of food ministry as a central part of their faith. In fact, when the gunman showed up on August 5, many members of the gurdwara were busy preparing food for a *langar,* a meal to which everyone is invited.

By joining in this shared ministry, Christ Our Savior members were able to express solidarity with their Sikh neighbors, offering them some much needed comfort in a time of sorrow. As Pastor Tom Kent writes:

> The outcome of shared projects across faith communities has led us all to grow in learning about one another. As families of different faiths worked together in the common cause of caring for the hungry, bridges were built and relationships begun. A new level of respect and perhaps more important, trust was established between our faith communities.

This trust between communities is one of the most important fruits of inter-religious work. A foundation of trust, built on years of involvement with the local communities, put members of Christ Our Savior in the position to support their Sikh neighbors, especially in their time of greatest need.

This is just one of the many success stories that this volume celebrates. Lutherans across North America are engaging in shared projects, conversations, and meals with our sisters and brothers from other faith traditions. These stories should encourage more congregations to follow suit; as both Mark Swanson (Chapter One) and Paul Rajashekar (Chapter Four) have pointed out, inter-religious work is essential to being Christian in a multi-religious world. Not only do we have more neighbors from other faiths in our midst here in North America, we also are more intimately aware of Christians who live in minority communities in Africa and Asia.

But inter-religious work is not merely a modern phenomenon, it is in the Bible, too. The Lutherans of Christ Our Savior are carrying out the lessons that Jesus taught us in his parable of the Good Samaritan, a story well known to us all.

The Good Samaritan: A Biblical Basis for Inter-Religious Action?

The story of the Good Samaritan may not seem, at first glance, to be about inter-religious work at all. A person is beaten and left to die. Ignored by several individuals, he is finally cared for by a Samaritan, who takes him to an inn and pays for him to be restored to health. In popular understanding, being a "Samaritan" is simply being a good person, one who looks out for others. But if we look closely, there is more to learn from this story from Luke. The parable arises in response to a question about what it means to be someone's neighbor.

> Jesus replied, "A man was going down from Jerusalem to Jericho, and fell into the hands of robbers, who stripped him, beat him, and went away, leaving him half dead. Now by chance a priest was going down that road; and when he saw him, he passed by on the other side. So likewise a Levite, when he came to the place and saw him, passed by on the other side. But a Samaritan while travelling came near him; and when he saw him, he was moved with pity. He went to him and bandaged his wounds, having poured oil and wine on them. Then he put him on his own animal, brought him to an inn, and took care of him. The next day he took out two denarii, gave them to the innkeeper, and said, 'Take care of him; and when I come back, I will repay you whatever more you spend'" (Luke 10:30-35, NRSV).

Scholars from the early church fathers through Martin Luther and up to the present have drawn many important lessons from this parable, which teaches us that the meaning of neighborliness is to act with mercy. What interests me here, however, is that a Samaritan was an adherent of a religion very much like Judaism, but different enough to be despised by most of Jesus' audience in Israel. Without question, Jesus is teaching his disciples (and us) that neighborliness extends across religious lines. We are to help one another, take care of the poor, and heal the sick regardless of their religious affiliation. Further, we can be inspired by the good works of our neighbors from other faiths, who occasionally may teach us how to be more compassionate and caring. In so many ways, the parable of the Good Samaritan exemplifies the promise of inter-religious work.

But I also want to suggest that, through its silence, this story presents the uncomfortable side of inter-religious work. In this story, the Samaritan, the Levite, and even the wounded man do not talk with one another. There is caring and healing, but there is no dialogue.

In contrast, Lutheran experiences of inter-religious work almost always include both action and dialogue, even if it is informal. And it is the combination of words and deeds that often presents us with the greatest challenge. Again, Christ Our Savior provides an example. When doing a food pack for the floods in Pakistan with a local Islamic society, Pastor Kent recalls, "to our embarrassment we had not provided a place for evening prayers on Friday for the Muslims in attendance." But the embarrassment inspired a desire to learn more about their neighbors. Pastor Kent's congregation now engages in information sessions on Sikhism, Islam, and other faiths. Further, the congregation discovered that learning cannot continue in only one direction; Pastor Kent clarified, "We are finding as we learn more about one another's faiths we are also driven to learn more about ours."

WHY DO INTER-RELIGIOUS ACTIVITIES WORK?

In surveys conducted by the Pluralism Project (pluralism. org/interfaith), "relationship-building" was the number one purpose of inter-religious activities. "Education" and "dialogue" were next in line, close runners-up.

"Service" and "spiritual development" ranked fourth and fifth as the reasons why people engage in inter-religious activities.

As a teacher, I am not surprised to hear this response. One of my main goals in the classroom is to have students question their own presumptions as they learn about the history and culture of others. This is all well and good in the university classroom, where students expect to be challenged, but the same experience has a different effect in the church. To the extent that members of our congregations come to church seeking reassurance in a frightening world, inter-religious work can present a challenge, even a threat to their understanding of theology.

This challenge is two-fold. First, while the actions of the Good Samaritan demonstrate the common humanity that is at the core of inter-religious work, discussions reveal the differences among religions. We may prefer to focus on the similarities among faiths—and there are a great many to find! Differences are uncomfortable and even embarrassing. Second, differences among faiths may cause us to ask uncomfortable questions about our own faith commitments. Using a fellowship hall to pack food or care packages for suffering Muslims in Pakistan is fairly non-controversial, but it is much harder to devote part of that hall for Muslim worship, as noted in Case Studies 1, "A Prayerful Place." If we do so, are we saying that it is okay to be a Muslim? That it's just as good as being a Lutheran? All the Good Samaritan did was take the time to show mercy to the beaten man; he was not forced to question his core faith commitments.

This concern is widely shared by those who begin the process of engaging their neighbors of other faiths. Rev. Susan Strouse of First United Lutheran Church in San Francisco recalled a discussion with a member of a congregation she was serving shortly after the attacks of September 11, 2001. Like many congregations, this one was responding to 9/11 by holding forums "to both study other religions and meet with adherents of those traditions." Rev. Strouse continues:

> After our session on Hinduism, one of the participants, "Elsie," asked if she could talk to me about something that was bothering her. She began by stating how much she was enjoying the study of Hinduism. But she was worried that if she accepted a Hindu's path as valid, she would be "betraying Jesus." We talked about her concerns. I reassured her that, given her firm foundation in Christianity, an exploration of other faiths would not endanger her soul. Afterwards, when I reflected on the incident, I realized that the encounter with a real live adherent of Hinduism had precipitated Elsie's dilemma and I wondered if Elsie had not raised an important issue for Christians today.

As a scholar of Islamic history, I have led many similar discussions in congregations, and occasionally I hear the same reaction. Just last year, after a series I led at my own church, Grace Lutheran in State College, Pennsylvania, an elderly member (whom I will call "Janet") spoke to me, clearly upset. Janet also had enjoyed greatly the chance to learn more about Islam, and, while she had no concerns about "betraying Jesus," her friends did. In fact, one of her long-time friends was so angry with her for attending my sessions that she threatened to cut off communication with Janet if she continued to learn more about Islam. I agree with Rev. Strouse, that "Elsie" had raised an important issue. Inter-religious work is challenging to our sense of faith precisely because, as Rev. Kent also pointed out, it is difficult simply to take in knowledge about another person's faith without it having an effect on our own.

In this chapter, I want to explore a few different dimensions of inter-religious work as a challenge. My goal is not to resolve these conundrums for the reader, but rather to try to understand their roots and their implications. In my mind, these concerns arise not from an incorrect or incomplete understanding of Christian theology; rather, they are genuine attempts to resolve what appear to be contradictions in Christian doctrine. Specifically, I am interested in addressing three key areas of the faith: our perception of God, our perception of ourselves, and ethical action in the world. In all of them a paradox arises because of a simple logical proposition: If our way is right, then how can other ways not be wrong?

Question Number 1: One God or Different Gods?

When the apostle Paul entered Athens, he saw many temples and shrines to all the gods and goddesses of the Greek pantheon, and he famously rejected them all. In Acts 17 we read:

> Then Paul stood in front of the Areopagus and said, 'Athenians, I see how extremely religious you are in every way. For as I went through the city and looked carefully at the objects of your worship, I found among them an altar with the inscription, "To an unknown god." What therefore you worship as unknown, this I proclaim to you. The God who made the world and everything in it, he who is Lord of heaven and earth, does not live in shrines made by human hands, nor is he served by human hands, as though he needed anything, since he himself gives to all mortals life and breath and all things (Acts 17:22-25, NRSV).

There are many interesting aspects to this story, but what I want to point out here is Paul's perception of God—it is not some personal god unique to Jews like Paul, but rather a universal God, one that the Athenians are worshiping without even knowing it—as he says, the "Lord of heaven and earth." In this perception, there can be no separate God of the Jews, God of the Athenians, and God of the Christians. Rather, all who worship "the God who made the world and everything in it" worship the same being.

So, here is our first question: Do we all worship the same God? On the one hand, we are taught that the Christian God is triune: "God in three persons, blessed Trinity" as the old hymn goes. Jesus, our Savior, is a vital part of this godhead, and worship of him is unique to Christians. But on the other hand, the notion of God described by Paul is one that would be completely familiar to Jews, Muslims and people of many other faiths. God is the being who "gives to all mortals life and breath and all things."

This latter insight has caused some theologians to abandon attempts to convert Muslims and Jews to Christianity, since they adhere to precisely the very notion of God to which Paul (a Jew) is calling the Athenians. In fact, the name for God in Arabic (*Allah*) is related to the name for God in Hebrew (*Elohim*).[1] Some go farther, opening themselves up to other possibilities. Rev. Strouse explored just this issue in her D.Min. thesis, "Passing Over and Coming Back: What does it mean to be a Christian in today's inter-religious world?" She has attended many inter-religious events and feels strongly that some of our liturgical practices and even readings from the New Testament can wrongly exclude members of other faiths. She writes about an inter-religious service she attended:

> As the priest read the passage from John's gospel, in which Jesus says, "I am the way, the truth and the life; no one comes to the Father but by me," I heard them through the ears of my friend who is Jewish. I had preached on that same text many times, especially at funerals, but hearing it this time was such a powerful epiphany that I hesitated to go up to receive Holy Communion. It felt rude, exclusionary, and offensive. Again, it was the human encounter that revealed the dilemma. The question of what it means to be a Christian in an interfaith world is not one that only the laity wrestles with.

Throughout her writing, Rev. Strouse emphasizes that inter-religious work poses a "dilemma," a set of issues that everyone must work through. Like Rajashekar (Chapter Four), she does not insist that Lutherans all respond in the same way, but suggests that engaging with people who belong to other faiths does pose real challenges. For her part, Rev. Strouse now changes the translation of Gospel passages that she understands to be anti-Semitic.

> The use of the words "the Jews" in John's gospel has been the root of much anti-Semitic thinking and action throughout history. As much as we try to teach the reasons for John's condemning language, too much damage has been done. I always change "the Jews" to "the Temple authorities" and believe that it is the only responsible thing to do.

As for her own faith, Rev. Strouse answers, "I can honestly say that my commitment to Christ has become much stronger. I am grounded in Christianity, while also learning from the wisdom of other traditions."

---

1 Our English word "God" comes from German, not from any of the languages of the Bible.

Not all pastors (or congregants) are comfortable with delving into the meanings of the original Greek text of the Gospels, or with offering alternative translations, however, preferring other ways to solve this dilemma. For many, Paul's proclaiming of the gospel to the Athenians is not a recognition of an inter-religious world, but an inspiration to missionize, to win souls for Christ. The author of Acts tells us that most Athenians scoffed at Paul's message, but that a few listened and were baptized.

Historically, these earliest converts would probably not be recognizable to us as Christians. After all, this event took place centuries before the Christian church decided (at the Council of Nicaea and elsewhere) just what a Christian theology of God entailed. Nonetheless, Paul's experience two thousand years ago is strikingly similar to that of Rev. Ronald Nelson, who ran a Christian radio program in Central Africa back in 1965, a program that continues to this day. This radio program was broadcast in Fulani, a Central African language whose speakers, according to Rev. Nelson, are "at least 95 percent Muslim." As a result of these broadcasts, wrote Rev. Nelson,

> Several thousand Fulani have become believers and they gather in villages to protect one another as well as for fellowship. Such villages exist in Cameroon, Nigeria, Central

HOW SOME OTHER RELIGIONS VIEW GOD

Judaism: " Hear, O Israel: The LORD is our God, the LORD alone. You shall love the LORD your God with all your heart, and with all your soul, and with all your might" (Deuteronomy 6:4-5, NRSV).

Islam: "God is one, God the everlasting. He has neither borne nor been born, and nothing is like Him" (Qur'an, Surat al-Ikhlas).

Christianity: "I believe in God, the Father almighty, creator of heaven and earth. I believe in Jesus Christ, God's only Son, our Lord, who was conceived by the Holy Spirit . . ." (Apostles' Creed).

Hinduism: "I am the origin or seed of all beings, O Arjuna. There is nothing, animate or inanimate, that can exist without Me" (Bhagavad Gita 10:39).

Fulani radio station developed with the help of Pastor Ronald Nelson.

African Republic, and Chad. They are not affiliated with any denomination, but organize annual international meetings. Besides visiting several of those villages, twice I have stayed a month and taught in one of the villages. In 2012 there were two adult classes and two school-age classes. They housed and fed me. The day I was to leave, they said, "We are already lonely." Most of them read Arabic script rather than Roman script, so the Bible in Fulani is being transcribed into Arabic script and will be available in 2014. They do not yet practice baptism or communion, but some have wanted to be baptized privately and it was my privilege to baptize five.

Like Paul, Rev. Nelson has spent his life reaching out to non-Christians, many of whom listen though only a few are baptized. Rev. Nelson's experiences remind us that for many Lutherans the world over, inter-religious is a way of life because they are minorities in a larger multi-religious environment.

But Rev. Nelson's interaction with religious others has not been limited to his trips abroad, nor is his experience a one-way street, since

he has also been changed through his long years of living in Africa. In fact, his experience and knowledge of the local language has made him an invaluable resource with Muslim Fulani communities in the United States. Long before Boko Haram kidnapped Muslim girls in Nigeria, these Muslims faced similar violence in the Central African Republic. Rev. Nelson writes that he was asked to

Pastor Nelson with Gomana village children.

aid some of these refugees due to his knowledge and experience:

Because of that background, I was asked in 2012 to help with two Fulani refugee families in Oregon. They are refugees because the Central African Republic government has been unable to control bandits. Their most lucrative practice is to kidnap children and hold them for ransom, and the favorite target is the Fulani because they have cattle and can sell a few to buy back their children. Hundreds of families have fled. Two families were transported to Oregon by Catholic Relief Services. One family has six children, the other seven. But they do not know English. There is one Wycliffe couple there who knows the Fulani language, but they make frequent trips back to Africa, so help was sorely needed. The children got registered in schools and health services were assured. Portland provided excellent housing for them.

After I had been with those families a few days, one of the fathers said, "It appears that we are relatives since we speak the same language and you know us so well." Since my return to North Dakota, he has called me six times, mostly just to greet but also to assure me that things are much better for them since my visit. They are still Muslim, but all of the important help for them has come from Christians, and that is making an impression.

Rev. Nelson's knowledge and expertise have put him in a position to be of great service to these immigrants, and the many phone calls attest to the esteem in which these families hold him. Yet his statement that "they are still Muslim" betrays a certain disappointment. He is clearly hoping for their conversion. And why not? If Jesus really is the "way, the truth, and the life," then do Muslims risk going to hell if they do not accept the Triune God?

How we view God has a direct impact on our inter-religious work. Historically, Christians have a long history of condemning religious others (along with members of varying Christian sects) to damnation. Yet today many Christians join Rev. Strouse in rejecting that past, finding wisdom in these non-Christian traditions. It is the conflict of what God expects from us that perhaps caused "Elsie" to feel that she was "betraying Jesus." But is this really a conflict? Does acknowledging that there is truth in Hinduism, Buddhism, Islam, or other traditions take away from the truth of Christianity? I do not believe so, and it may be more fruitful to regard these conflicting views not as a contradiction (for which there can only be two opposing solutions), but as a paradox.

A paradox seems to defy common sense because it holds that two apparently contradictory statements are both true. As Darrell Jodock once said to me, "The purpose of paradoxes is not to obscure the truth but to invite us to see it more deeply." Like all religions, Christianity is full of these paradoxes. Communion is a good example: Bread and wine are both real bread and wine, but also Christ's body and blood. Likewise, we know that God is one, yet three. Perhaps most central is the paradox of the cross, laid out for us in a memorable passage about the "foolishness of God" in 1 Corinthians 1:18-31.

LUTHERANS EMBRACING THE PARADOX

Paul Rajashekar addresses the theological foundation for Lutheran inter-religious work in Chapter Four.

Many more examples of congregations engaging in inter-religious work are covered by Carol Schersten LaHurd in Chapter Two.

For more resources on inter-religious relations, see the appendices to this book, including links to online materials at elca.org/ecumenical.

To my mind, we can treat inter-religious work as a paradox, engaging and honoring the religious faith of others, even while devoting ourselves to our Lutheran Christian traditions. Again, what I am rejecting here is the need to make an exclusive choice, to say that my conviction that I am saved by the grace of God somehow means that (a) I have nothing to learn from other religious traditions; (b) that accepting the truth of other faiths belittles the truth of my own; or that (c) God will save only those who believe in this one Lutheran way. As a paradox, I accept the logical confusion that these propositions entail, but I press on anyway, clinging to the wonder of God's action through religious others and open to learning more about God by engaging this mystery: Our Lutheran faith exists in a world of many religions.

Rev. Jane Buckley-Farlee, pastor of Trinity Lutheran in Minneapolis explains her perception of this paradox in this way:

> In the many conversations we have had with our Muslim brothers and sisters, it becomes clear that God is bigger than we ever will be able to imagine and that no particular theology can explain all of God. When we come together in honest conversation, we each grow stronger in our own faith, yet with a deeper understanding and respect for the others' faith. We become even more appreciative of our own faith's lens for understanding God, and our views of God are expanded.

This view comes from a distinct set of experiences that I will describe further, but Rev. Buckley-Farlee sums it up nicely when she says, "God is big enough for all of us."

A Second Question: How Do We View Ourselves in a Multi-Religious World?

Fundamentally, the previous discussion is a theoretical one. After all, few have seen God and no one can know the mind of God. It is this physical world that we inhabit, and it is here that we must live out our lives. Most religious traditions agree that this material world is not the complete reality of existence, but it is all that our limited senses can know.

This is certainly an important issue, but it is not the one I want to address here. My aim in this section is to understand our perception of ourselves within this material existence. Part of the attraction of the Lutheran church is that it is so familiar, in two senses of that term. On the one hand, I treasure the liturgy, common hymns, and shared activities with my fellow Lutherans. But on the other hand, it is *literally* familiar. I have several Lutheran pastors in my family, as does my wife. Seven out of eight of my son's great-grandparents were Lutheran, and they were all of German extraction.

I do not speak of my "Lutheran family" in some sort of abstract way—my family is almost all Lutheran! Our whiteness is reflected in our church; the ELCA has been over 96 percent white for many years and continues to be so. In contrast, the United States is only 63 percent non-Hispanic white, a number that is dropping. At the same time, the Lutheran church is growing in Africa and Asia while it shrinks in Europe and North America. There are now almost as many Lutherans in Ethiopia, Tanzania, and Indonesia as there are in the United States.

COUNTRY	LUTHERANS
Germany	12,202,382
United States	6,671,842
Sweden	6,500,000
Ethiopia	6,355,383
Tanzania	5,825,312
Indonesia	5,812,489
Denmark	4,430,643
Finland	4,146,056
Norway	3,847,098
India	3,538,912

And so the uncomfortable second paradox arises from this difference, the strange distinction between self and other. When we look around on a Sunday morning, we see ourselves—yes, people of different ages and stages of life, but fundamentally people like us. We do not normally go to mosques, synagogues, or *gurdwaras*, but when we do we see others, people not like us. Inter-religious activities therefore cause us to enter unfamiliar, uncomfortable territory. It is not only the theological questions we must face, but also issues of ethnic and racial discrimination. Sometimes, our attitude toward religious difference can mask unresolved racial prejudice.

Sociologically, prejudices function as a way to define ourselves. Put another way, we know we are Lutherans because we are not like what we presume Muslims, Jews, or Hindus to be. Inter-religious encounters threaten this clear distinction by making the other more familiar to us. Once we gain knowledge about these traditions, it is no longer possible to say, "We do not worship idols, like Hindus," or "We do not blindly follow religious law like Muslims and Jews." But this raises a second uncomfortable question: By learning about others, do we lose our sense of ourselves?

Consider the fact that inter-religious encounters are not a normal part of our worship experience. In fact, they often arise out of some crisis in the world. The cases surveyed above are typical: an attack on Sikh neighbors in Milwaukee, programs on inter-religious learning as a response to 9/11, helping to settle immigrants from Central Africa. From Somalis in Minneapolis to Hindus in Atlanta, our experience of religious diversity can appear to be an interruption in the natural order of things, an unwelcome change.

And yet, that diversity has often been there all along. My home-town of Valparaiso, Indiana, is also home to a synagogue, Temple Israel, now prominently located on Evans Avenue. But I was shocked and a bit embarrassed to discover that this congregation existed in Valparaiso, in one form or another, for over sixty years before the synagogue was constructed in 1986.[2] Times change, sometimes for the better. What was once hidden away in the upper floors of a backstreet storefront is now a prominent part of the community.

The fact is that North America has always been a religiously diverse world. Not only did Native Americans present a wide variety of religious beliefs, early settlers from Europe also brought varying ideas of faith. Columbus himself likely had Muslims on his crew, as they were among the most skilled navigators of that time. Africans captured and brought to work plantations as slaves already in the sixteenth century also brought along their religious diversity, including at least 10 percent who were Muslims before being forcibly converted to Christianity. Lutheran Germans, Swedes, and Norwegians were part of a different story, bringing their home traditions to the United States when they came here to establish a new life.

Formerly serving as interim pastor in a small ELCA congregation in Indianapolis, Rev. Bonnie Sparks, ordained in the United Church of

_____

2 www.templeisrael.info/about-us.aspx

Christ, is deeply aware of this heritage and of the necessity to transcend it. Salem Lutheran Church has been in Indianapolis for nearly 180 years.[3] During that time, demographics have shifted dramatically, and what was once an ethnically uniform congregation has broadened considerably. Rev. Sparks writes:

> At the time of the 175th anniversary, members were chronologically-gifted descendants of northern European Protestants. In the opinion of some, Salem would probably die away after the anniversary. Someone forgot to tell God, however. The following year African nationals started arriving at Salem. Now half of the congregation are African nationals who are active in the life of the church and serve in leadership positions. What is amazing is that this transition happened seamlessly—truly a God thing!

The African nationals that Rev. Sparks refers to are friends of a Pentecostal Congolese refugee who found the church on the internet and then proceeded to invite his friends to join. At first glance, this is not a story of inter-religious relations. The African nationals were certainly different from the older members of the congregations, but they were Christians. As Rev. Sparks explains, however, these new members brought along their own inter-religious experiences.

> In Africa, Christian-Muslim relationships are different from the United States. Both faiths, for the most part, interact in peace and harmony. (We have one ESL [English as a Second language] student whose mother is Roman Catholic and father is Muslim.) African Salemites brought this ideology with them.

Salem is a success story, but this success came at a cost. Its aging congregation reflected its core of committed members who tried to keep tradition alive. Race, class, and culture divided this core of members from much of the rest of Indianapolis. To open themselves up to change meant losing some of the identity markers that made the church so familiar. This loss seemed too great, until Africans moved in, embraced Lutheran Christianity, and made it their own. These new members broached the divide, founding new ministries to engage the surrounding community. Throughout our country, racial, class, and ethnic divisions abound, and violence seems to reign. We do not have to wait for the miracle of a Con-

---

3 In 2015, Pastor Sparks retired, and Douglas Mmari was called to serve Salem's congregation and also to serve as Salem's Minister of African Development, a synodically-authorized worship center with the African national faith community in Indianapolis.

Salem Lutheran Church, Indianapolis, Indiana, participates in the Festival of Faiths, sponsored by the Center for Interfaith Cooperation at the Veterans Memorial Plaza. Here the Salem group is in front of the stage. Photo by Devoe Slisher.

At the First Annual Harvest Festival on October 12, 2014, members of Salem Lutheran who have immigrated from Zimbabwe and students and tutors from the Salem ELSL class meet. Standing on the far right are Salem Outreach chaiperson Fred Freeman and Pastor Bonnie Sparks. Photo by Douglas Mmari.

golese refugee to arrive at our doorsteps to begin reaching out, like the Good Samaritan, to the communities in our midst.

Pastor Sparks writes that "Salem is unique from every church in the Indiana-Kentucky Synod and probably from almost every church in the ELCA." Yet the fact is that many other churches are facing similar crises—aging membership, fewer engaged members. It seems to be a strange paradox indeed that inter-religious engagement could actually help a church through these trying times.

Back in Milwaukee, Pastor Kent shared,

> Over twenty years ago Christ Our Savior was recovering from a difficult time when it had lost over half its members following controversy over a former pastor. It had just completed a building program to provide space it no longer needed given the starkly declined membership. There was widespread fear and despair among members about its debt, its future and viability as a congregation.

Like Salem, Christ Our Savior chose to engage rather than to shut its doors. As Pastor Kent recalls, the congregation "opened up two acres of land for the Hmong community in Milwaukee to garden and offered spare space in its building for an office for Interfaith Caregiving Network. Both events helped Christ Our Savior move from a mentality of scarcity to abundance, seeing the assets it had to share in the midst of its looming debt."

Coming back to the Good Samaritan parable, it strikes me that neither Salem nor Christ Our Savior is the Good Samaritan, with money and time enough to stop and heal the sick. Frankly, they were a lot more like the man on the side of the road: battered and bleeding, ready to curl up and die. But rather than die, they chose to open themselves to the care of others, even those who belong to different faiths.

So the answer to this question of identity is fairly simple: Inter-religious work is transformative. To some extent, we will lose ourselves. But as Pastor Kent notes, what changed at Christ Our Savior was a "mentality" not a reality. It found riches amidst its debt and hope in decline. So, we could also say that both Salem and Christ Our Savior did not really lose themselves. Rather, they came to know themselves, or at least to view themselves, differently.

The great nineteenth-century scholar Max Müller famously quipped, "Who knows one religion, knows none." In other words, learning about other religions can help us to know our own. This may be part of the mystery as to why we believe in "one holy catholic and apostolic church," yet God has placed the church in a world of many religions. How we respond to this strange gift is up to us.

A Final Question: How to Respond Ethically to Our Neighbors?

Healing the sick was one of Jesus' key ministries, and his healing was offered freely to all. This is not always the case. As Rev. Robert Ove tells us from his experience as a missionary in Nepal, "We had a clinic and only asked a fee for those who could afford it. The Hindus and Buddhists were surprised, as their priest wanted *bacshesh* (money) up front before they would pray for a healing." The actions of the priests here seem wrong because they do not conform to our notion of *agape,* of loving without hope or expectation of getting something in return. Again, this was precisely the love demonstrated by the Good Samaritan.

Rev. Ove recommends following Jesus' example and practicing this form of selfless love wherever we are. He writes, "It will work at home or in the mission field." Yet here, "at home," we do not find a world that regards this truth as self-evident. Not only is health care expensive, so are many other aspects of daily living. Yes, there are free clinics in many places, but where I live in central Pennsylvania, the clinic for free dental services is overwhelmed with 1,400 people on the waiting list.

Here, then, is my third question: Just how far does love go? If inter-religious action changes our sense of self and we start to identify with the immigrants, the refugees from war and famine, does inter-religious action mean we also identify with their struggles? Put in terms of the Good Samaritan parable, does a Good Samaritan have a responsibility to make the road safer in order to stop robbery in the first place?

This is certainly the experience of Salem Lutheran Church in Indianapolis. In receiving new members, Salem not only revitalized a dying congregation, it also developed new ministries to the surrounding community, a community that reflects the diversity of many urban areas. Again, Rev. Sparks writes:

> In January 2013, Salem Lutheran Church in Indianapolis began an ESL (English as a Second Language) program. Salem hired a lead teacher who happened to be a devout Muslim. Salem provided a support staff of a dozen individuals consisting of learning assistants and transportation staff. Over

The Spring 2015 ESL students hold up their certificates as they wrap up. Photo by Devoe Slisher.

fifty students from five continents have passed through the program. This combined group represents Christianity, Islam, Buddhism, Hinduism, Shinto, and Confucianism. Part of class includes cultural understanding, and religions seemed to be the center of these discussions although a number of students were not particularly active in religious practices.

With this engagement, however, also comes the real pain of the violence and poverty experienced in urban environments everywhere. What began as a class to teach English has now turned into a path to legal, health, and other services. Rev. Sparks has also served as an intermediary between the police and local communities. These communities have been drawn together by tragedy, as Rev. Sparks explains:

> Last year our teacher's brother was killed in a workplace robbery. Four months later another innocent young man from the mosque was killed as he got out of his car when a drug deal went wrong at the other end of his apartment parking lot. Every Sunday, Salem now prays for the end to violence in our city and for God's peace to rest in the hearts of sisters and brothers at the mosque. In August, Salem invited members of the mosque to join with Salem to pray together during Night Out Against Crime.

The word Salem is related both to the Hebrew *shalom* and the Arabic *salam*; it means peace. With these new ministries, Salem Lutheran is embodying the love of Christ and bringing a measure of God's peace to urban Indianapolis. But while Salem's experiences are unique, its position in a diverse world is not.

In the next chapter, Paul Rajashekar describes a "relational theology of Christ" that challenges us to understand God's work in a multi-religious world. Similarly, in the previous chapter, Carol Schersten LaHurd suggests that "as friendships develop and sacred scripture is explored, the study becomes spiritual and relational as well as intellectual." I find help in understanding this notion of "relational" activity through the philosopher Maria Lugones, who talks about the need for transformative love in today's world; she explains that this love is tied up with our sense of self and other. Her notion of "loving perception" requires us to enter the world of another person so profoundly that we start to see the world through their eyes: We even start to see ourselves through their eyes.

What we see, of course, can make us mighty uncomfortable. Consider the legal, but unethical, practice of "payday loans," a lending practice that can saddle poor people with unbearable debt. This subject came up in an English class taught at Salem Lutheran Church. Rev. Sparks recalls:

> One student brought up pawn brokers/payday loans. I explained how these companies operate and why the students should never deal with this business. One student exclaimed, "That is not the way of Islam!" I responded, "That is not the way of Christianity either."

I find this example interesting because it so beautifully demonstrates Lugones' notion. By holding the ESL class in the first place, Rev. Sparks started to see Indianapolis through the eyes of her students. But the student went further, suggesting that such practices would not be tolerated in a Muslim country, and that therefore something was wrong with the United States as a "Christian country." Here, Rev. Sparks started to see herself through the eyes of her students, and what is important to them started to become important to her.

Rev. Sparks did not stop with her response that our separation of church and state means that many actions can be legal but not necessarily moral. In fact, after the 2014 Kentucky-Indiana Synod Assembly, she could be seen with other members of her congregation picketing outside of a payday loan office.

This sort of engaged witness might be considered by some to be unseemly, yet when we see the world through the eyes of our neighbors, we see a world of injustice that can no longer be ignored. When we view ourselves in this world, we may feel compelled to do things differently. We might well respond as Rev. Strouse did with her radical openness to others by revisiting the translation of scriptural passages. Or, we could follow the example of Rev. Buckley-Farlee who serves a church in Minneapolis in a neighborhood that is "the home of the largest group of Somalis outside of Somalia and has been nicknamed 'Little Mogadishu.'" For the past twenty-five years, Trinity Lutheran has hosted a weekly meal with their Muslim Somali neighbors, and Rev. Buckly-Farlee writes: "Each week we gather as Christians and Muslims around the table, share announcements, sing 'Johnny Appleseed' and end with 'bis-me-lah'" which is Arabic for "in God's name."

As with Salem in Indianapolis, Trinity in Minneapolis has become home to a variety of outreach services, even providing space for Muslims to worship when one of the mosques burned down on New Year's Day. But what are the costs of this focus on ethical action, service, and love for neighbor? Does it distract Lutherans from their real calling—or worse, could it be "betraying Jesus" as "Elsie" seemed to suggest?

Rev. David Moe of Faith Lutheran Church in Sun City, California, seems to think so. He writes: "I believe the sole source of authority to be the person of Jesus Christ. . . . Christian authority is the central issue in inter-religious relations." Rev. Moe is not suggesting that there is anything wrong with service to our neighbors, only that it should not detract from the more important activity of caring for their souls. Rev. Robert Ove, the missionary to Nepal mentioned above, appears to agree, though he prefers to show love rather than to "use aggressive evangelism to prove that we were the *only* way to God."

Rev. Ove regards Muslims as unbelievers, however. He writes:

> I have Muslims friends and I never tell them they are going to hell unless they convert! It may take a while, but they are asking why I am so loving and never badger them. One has started to read more of the New Testament to find out for himself. I could have turned them off by attempting to evangelize them. I didn't have to! God was doing it, and I left it in his hands. It works! It is much easier to "convert" friends than enemies!

Rev. Ove's approach to the self–other conundrum is also illuminated by Lugones' theory of "loving perception." For Lugones, the self and the other respond within a world of human interaction. For Rev. Ove, the concepts of self and other are a bit illusory, since God is the real actor. We are merely vessels for God's action. For Lugones, loving perception results in seeing the world through the eyes of the other, which could result in ethical action—such as picketing a payday loan office. But for Ove, who believes that Muslims and people of other faiths may well be going to hell, ethical action means encouraging them to convert to Christianity. These need not be exclusive propositions, as it is always right to tend to the needs of others, but how we resolve this paradox will affect how we engage in inter-religious work.

I cannot condemn Rev. Moe and Rev. Ove for their desire that all would know the love of Christ which so obviously plays a significant role in their lives. Indeed, I admire their service and engagement with our multi-religious world. But I must confess that I am more drawn to Lugones' theory and Rajashekar's theology (Chapter Four), because they pay more attention to the experience of religious others. If we're open to it, this experience is often quite surprising. For example, Rev. Kent recalls an eventful evening, when a member of the Islamic Society of Milwaukee came to Christ Our Savior Lutheran Church to tell them about Islam.

This cannot have been easy. On the one hand, everyone knows that Americans have generally negative views of Islam.[4] On the other hand, no one person, no matter how well-read, can hope to respond on behalf of a large and complex religious tradition. When we invite Muslims, Buddhists or others into our churches, though, these are precisely the sort of questions they often face. Pastor Kent writes:

> One member asked the presenter about the Muslim understanding of heaven or afterlife, asking whether Muslims believed they would be the only ones there. The presenter responded saying, "First, I cannot imagine our God wanting to separate himself from part of his creation. Second, if you people are not there, I am not sure it would be heaven."

In this case, the presenter took a universal question that Muslim theologians have struggled with for years and personalized it—not what "Islam says," but what he as a Muslim could imagine and how he would

---

4 Including 47 percent of Protestant pastors, as reported in *Ministry Today* magazine (www.ministrytodaymag.com/index.php/ministry-news/65-news-main/18892-protestant-pastors-have-negative-view-of-islam).

feel. This was not the question that the church member asked, but it is the answer she needed.

If we were to answer the question, could we imagine an answer like this one? We often think of all creation yearning for God, but we rarely reverse that, and think of God as yearning for creation, not wanting to be separated from it. But the Muslim representative's second answer is even more surprising. In it, he ascribes to his Christian audience a place in heaven, recognizing them as fully ethical human beings, apart from theological differences. Pastor Kent wrote that "there was not a dry eye in the house."

Once again, listening to people of other faiths—even thinking about listening to them—causes us to reflect more deeply on our own faith commitments. That reflection can raise uncomfortable questions, but we need not face these questions alone, especially as more and more Lutherans engage in this work.

Conclusion: Opening the Door

We might disagree on the purpose and ultimate effects of inter-religious encounters, but all of us writing this book believe strongly that the risk is worth taking. I would even suggest that inter-religious encounters can make us more ethical people: As our definition of "neighbor" expands, we become aware of issues of injustice that face these neighbors.

I can think of no better example of how to open doors than this one from East Lansing, Michigan. This is an example of literal neighbors, since University Lutheran Church (serving Michigan State) and the Islamic Center of East Lansing are right next door to one another. The story was sent in by Pastor Fred Fritz, though it was written by Asim Ansari and reflects his experience.

It seems that the parking lot for the Islamic Center is just too small to accommodate all the worshippers at a typical Friday noon congregational prayer, and so by mutual agreement the congregations use each other's parking lots. This particular Friday, however, there were a lot of cars, and so Mr. Ansari and two of his cousins decided to drop by the church after prayers to express their appreciation for the arrangement. It is evident from his telling that this was his first time in the church, and it took a good deal of courage to walk in. In his words:

> As we walked back to the car, parked in the church parking lot,
> I asked my cousins how they felt about saying a little thank

you to the church goers for letting us use their lot and, being my wonderful cousins, of course they agreed. So we walked into this massive church, probably three times the size of the mosque and decided to find someone to thank. With a service going on, we dared not interrupt. Looking around, I knocked on the door labeled "office" and found myself staring at a slightly confused older gentleman sitting on his desk.

(knock knock)

"Hi...I hope I'm not bothering you, Um, I just wanted to talk to you, sir. Do you have a minute? May I come in?" I never thought saying thank you could feel so awkward. Confused, but welcoming, he invited us in. I explained how I was from Toronto and come here often to pray when visiting family, and that today, like most Fridays, we parked in their parking lot.

I could see his face tense up a little, the shoulders hunched a bit further down, the lips sealed just a bit tighter, as he continued to listen. I continued, "And I know it's pretty full; but we just wanted to come in here and say Thank You. We really appreciate it."

I'll never forget the transformation on his face, the shoulders opened up, raised eyebrows a fitting sign of surprise followed by the biggest and most welcoming smile I'd seen, a smile that no mosque dweller could have matched that day. Two little words had changed the entire body language and atmosphere of the room. A beaming smile then explained how as today was Good Friday, they had their own special service going on, hence the "unusual clash" of parking. I hadn't even realized it was Good Friday, and it struck me, how even on such a holy Christian day, nothing was any different. Nothing had changed. Not only was the church larger in size from the mosque, but certainly, bigger in heart.

The three of us shook his hand, thanked him, walking out feeling a little better about ourselves. As we exited the church, I could see what were most likely church goers, patiently waiting at the entrance of the lot, waiting for the Muslims to leave so they could park and go attend their own service. *Subhan Allah* (God be praised).

From the many stories we have received, it seems that this experience is not at all unique: Opening the door is never easy, but almost always rewarding. While questions and concerns remain, the delight in opening the door of a mosque, a temple, an ashram, or a church and finding there a welcoming smile is an invaluable experience.

As for why God put us into a world of religious diversity, one possibility can be found in the Qur'an, where God points out that if he had wished, he could have made everyone of a single religion. But difference has a purpose: "O humankind, indeed We have created you from male and female and put you [in this world] as peoples and tribes that you may know one another" (Qur'an 49:13).

Perhaps this was the wisdom that Max Müller was channeling in his famous dictum. If we were unique in this world, we could not appreciate the gifts that we have. Likewise, if there were only Lutherans, or only Christians, we would not know how to value the gift of Jesus, God's only son made flesh. Yet it is also evident that we are not the only recipients of God's gifts and that God's handiwork is found throughout creation, even among people whose faiths differ from ours.

FOR DISCUSSION

1. Whom do you relate to in the Good Samaritan story? In what ways can you empathize with each different character in the story?

2. Which stories in this section did you find especially inspirational? What about them inspired you?

3. What do you think is at stake in inter-religious work? What are the risks and possible benefits as you see them? Are there possible risks and benefits mentioned in this chapter that are new to you?

4. What do you think is at stake in inter-religious work for your partners from other faiths? What risks and benefits exist for them in your view?

5. How can we best foster interactions with people of other faiths that minimize the risks and increase the benefits for all concerned?

Grounding Interfaith Engagement in Identity and Mission: Concordia College–Moorhead Creates Official Interfaith Engagement Statement

Dr. Jacqueline Bussie, Director, Forum on Faith and Life, Concordia College

It is August 2012, and Dr. Eboo Patel, founder and president of Interfaith Youth Core and Concordia's first Forum on Faith and Life guest speaker, has just given the fall convocation keynote. A mother and daughter sit in a faculty office and ask with genuine curiosity, "Why would a Lutheran school have a Muslim convocation speaker?" After repeatedly fielding this and similar questions related to Concordia's recent foray into interfaith dialogue, service, and cooperation, Concordia's President's Interfaith Advisory Council (PIAC)—made up of faculty, staff, administrators and students—decided to lead our community to answer this together in an articulate, mission-grounded, and theologically-informed way.

After a full year of word-smithing, student focus groups, faculty consultations, countless meetings, and broad-based consensus building, the end result was an official college interfaith engagement statement that we cherish for its connections both to our specific college mission and to the greater ELCA's values: "Concordia College practices interfaith cooperation because of its Lutheran dedication to prepare thoughtful and informed global citizens who foster wholeness and hope, build peace through understanding, and serve the world together." In March 2015, the faculty as a whole voted unanimously to approve the statement. The college president, admissions and advancement staff, students, and faculty now use the statement regularly as a crucial representation of our public interfaith identity.

Upon further reflection, we realized that the process of creating the statement had evoked fascinating and long overdue conversations. None of us will ever forget the meeting wherein an extraordinarily lively yet respectful debate broke out over the subordinate clause, "because of its Lutheran dedication...." Several Christian group members (Lutherans and others) argued for the milder subordinate conjunction "guided by," but—perhaps contrary to expectations—an atheist student and a Muslim faculty colleague argued adamantly for the unequivocal phrasing "because of." My

Muslim colleague passionately insisted, "I want to know that there will **always** be a place for me here . . . that I belong here because this place is Lutheran, not because some folks might possibly be 'guided' to create a space for me...or not." In the end, she persuaded everyone in the room. After the meeting was over, this same colleague—who after Patel had spoken at convocation had written me an email that said, "Thank you. That was the first time in sixteen years that I felt I truly belonged here"— thanked me merely for including her voice in the discussion. For many of us, the year-long conversation beautifully revealed to us the unity within our diversity. We witnessed our diversity being not erased, but reconciled.

Lessons learned? The process of creating a pluralism statement for your institution is as informative and necessary as the actual statement itself. We should not perceive interfaith engagement as an abandonment or dilution of heritage, identity, or mission, but instead as an enrichment and extension of our cherished values.

Can We Worship Together across Religious Traditions?

Students at Augustana College, Rock Island, show how young adults can take the lead.

Pastor Richard W. Priggie, Chaplain, Augustana College, Rock Island, Illinois

Several years after establishing an Interfaith Understanding Group on campus, student leaders at Augustana College, Rock Island, Illinois, approached me with a dilemma. They had organized themselves to work side-by-side as Christians, Jews, Muslims, and others in shared service projects. They met every Monday evening to share their faith journeys and try out faith practices, like fasting, together. Something still was missing, they told me, some sort of regular spiritual practice that they could experience together. What if they were to plan joint worship opportunities, they asked, where students could pray and light candles and sing and be nourished by spiritual readings, silence, and conversation?

While I was excited to support their energy and intention, I raised questions with them. Is "worship" a particularly Christian term, in a way that others would feel excluded by an invitation to worship together? Would Jews describe their weekly Shabbat service, for instance, as "worship"? Would Muslims label as "worship" their Friday prayers? Moreover, how could we be sure to fashion interfaith worship that would plumb the depths of our various spiritual traditions, thus avoiding a lowest-common-denominator experience, so concerned not to offend that no one is nourished, stimulated, or challenged?

After significant reflection and conversation, the students proposed to organize interfaith worship around a different *question* each time. They wanted to validate questioning as an important ingredient in a faithful life and felt that they could easily identify a set of questions that would engage all students, regardless of their faith background.

And so worship was planned that invited the campus community to come together around one pressing question each time, questions like these:

- How can I remain faithful to my own spiritual background and be open to guidance from many spiritual sources?

- What does it mean to be on a spiritual journey?

- Do you know your spiritual family tree?

- What do I love when I love my God?

- How can I become a steward of the earth?

Readings are chosen from the holy books of various traditions and from a wide spectrum of such respected elders as Elie Wiesel, Richard Rohr, and Gandhi. Poetry always seems to make its voice heard, and we generally sing a song or two from places committed to interfaith understanding like The Taizé Community in France. Students have drawn upon mystical resources, such as Rumi, the Sufi poet, to fashion beginning and ending litanies to be spoken together. There is significant silence in the middle and a time of conversation too, centering upon the question of the day.

The process is the key. Begin with young adults, wherever you can find them. Encourage them to bring friends to the planning from differing religious traditions. Start with their most urgent questions, what they most wonder about. Let them lead, while clergy and others help around the edges. Prepare to experience worship that will stretch your faith in creative, healthy ways and bind you together across religious differences.

Seminary Interfaith Learning: Beyond the Books to Engagement

Sara Trumm, program coordinator, A Center of Christian-Muslim Engagement for Peace and Justice (CCME), Lutheran School of Theology at Chicago

At A Center of Christian-Muslim Engagement for Peace and Justice (CCME), Lutheran School of Theology at Chicago (LSTC), we have many wonderful opportunities to build bridges of mutual understanding, respect, and cooperation among people of all faiths. As the seminary strives to prepare future leaders for ministry in a pluralistic context, knowing and learning from others despite or even because of our differences becomes essential to the educational and relational experience. The seminary has a long history of interfaith relationships and activities with a variety of faith traditions, including an annual commemoration and commitment service on the anniversary of the Kristallnacht pogrom in Nazi Germany. In particular, seminary students and other religious leaders learn from Islam in its breadth and depth, our Muslim neighbors in their rich diversity, and the history of relations between faith communities.

With our many interfaith partners in and around Chicago, nurturing and deepening relationships happens through shared events and activities. We are regularly welcomed to observe prayer, share a meal, and discuss with religious leaders, lay leaders, or even high school youth during small group mosque visits. The reflection and thoughtfulness necessary as participants ask or answer a question of the "other" is heightened when one is stripped of the commonly understood language within one's own faith tradition. Invitations to *iftar* (breaking of the fast) meals during Ramadan are plentiful as well. These larger group events give Christian participants a chance to receive the overwhelming hospitality of their Muslim neighbors as well as witness the dedication many Muslims have to a month of fasting. Within our own community, the presence of several Muslim students enriches class discussions and community events, as well as leading to friendships across religious lines.

A seminarian who attended an *iftar* event had these reflections: "The opportunity to share in an *iftar* meal with my Muslim brothers and sisters in Libertyville this past June was life-giving. I believe that we are all more holistic and healthy people when we not only engage in meaningful conversation with one another, but when we take the time to *experience* meaningful events together as well. Celebrating Ramadan together offered an opportunity for me to learn more about this holy season within Islam and how my Muslim brothers and sisters commemorate this time. As a future Christian pastor I feel called to continually share my life and experiences with my interfaith brothers and sisters that I might grow in my own worldview and become vulnerable to opportunities of experiencing God in new ways. We are stronger together, and I feel blessed to have opportunities for this kind of deep interfaith engagement."

Creative arts events also have provided comfortable settings for people from various faith traditions to come together and connect in meaningful and fun ways. The seminary and area congregations have hosted musical groups such as the Rose Ensemble from St. Paul, Minnesota, or the Maxwell Street Klezmer Band's Salaam-Shalom Project not only to have an interfaith audience tap their toes together to some wonderful sounds, but also to learn the history of music in interfaith communities living in harmony. Touring the Islamic gallery at the Art Institute of Chicago with a group of fifteen people representing ten different countries brought out some wonderful reflections about how our faith communities change and how they stay the same over time. Local playwright, Rohina Malik has a beautiful way of depicting very real issues in the lives of Muslim women. CCME was able to bring her play, *Unveiled* to campus in 2009, and hosted *Mecca Tales* in 2015. After being drawn into the personal lives of the characters, I witnessed interfaith audiences engage in extremely deep and emotion-filled discussion.

Area Christian congregations who are looking to educate themselves and build stronger communities have asked CCME for assistance in getting to know their Muslim neighbors. Often, this process begins with a series of lectures and small group discussions at adult forums or evening study programs. An introduction to Islam and conversation about why Christians should bother with interfaith interaction from a biblical perspective often begins the series. Six short documentary videos in the *Discover Islam* resource have proved extremely helpful to hear from Muslims about some of the most important (and controversial) issues facing American Christians about Islam. Muslim presenters co-lead some of the sessions. After the series is complete, congregations often then arrange for a mosque visit in their community or invite Muslims in the area to an event at their congregation. In some cases, Muslim community members have participated in the full series, giving valuable input about their personal experiences throughout.

More recently, a Muslim nurse who serves at a hospice care facility requested our help to provide a workshop for non-Muslim chaplains to learn about and gain confidence in caring for Muslim patients. The chaplains were periodically coming to her for advice. She saw a need in her own facility and quickly found out that other health care center chaplains were interested. Before long, we had one of our Muslim Ph.D. students preparing workshop sessions, and eight other Muslim partners responded immediately to our inquiry about whether they could help. We have now held three chaplaincy workshops! The response has been overwhelmingly positive, as not only do participants gain knowledge, but they are able to interact with so many wise Muslim leaders as they discuss intimate health care concerns and issues. We now are hoping to expand this program for nurses, social workers, and others in the health care field.

Day of Dialogue: Neighbors in Conversation around Shared Interests

Allen I. Juda, rabbi emeritus, Congregation Brith Sholom, Bethlehem, Pennsylvania, and chair, Day of Dialogue Planning Team

The Day of Dialogue, a program of the Institute for Jewish-Christian Understanding (IJCU) of Muhlenberg College, emerged from The Abrahamic Accord. As described in a 1993 IJCU brochure, "The Abrahamic Accord is an Episcopal/Jewish project aimed at bringing to the Christian and Jewish communities of America the remarkable changes which have occurred in academic theological dialogue during recent years. . . . The goal of the project is the transformation of Jewish-Christian relationships to reflect their common origin as the children of Abraham, to be expressed as an 'accord' founded upon that common origin and our common commitment to the gracious sovereignty of God." The Abrahamic Accord was brought to Muhlenberg College by Dr. Franklin Sherman, founding director of the Institute for Jewish-Christian Understanding, on May 17, 1993, and was subtitled "A Day of Dialogue."

Dr. Sherman continued to organize similar programs and took the name, Day of Dialogue, from The Abrahamic Accord. There have been approximately twenty programs since 1993, the most recent one taking place on April 19, 2015, at the Muslim Association of the Lehigh Valley. It was titled: "Strong Faith—Open Heart"; the focus question was, "How does a person cultivate and sustain a strong personal belief system and at the same time hold an open and compassionate attitude toward people of another faith?"

In the early years, the Day of Dialogue programs focused on issues of common concern between the Christian and Jewish communities. Among the early program highlights were

- "What Do Jews and Christians Believe Happens After You Die?" (1998);
- "Will Traditional Faith Survive in the 21st Century?" with a the keynote speaker and three local clergy respondents (2000); and
- "Is Your Religion Being Hijacked?" with a the keynote speaker and three local panelists (2002).

The 2002 program was noteworthy as the first Day of Dialogue occurring after 9/11 and the first including a Muslim panelist. Since 2002, each program has included the Muslim community, with several programs being held in local masjids (mosques). Both in substance and symbolism, as the crescent joined the star of David and the cross on the brochures, the Day of Dialogue became more inclusive of the Muslim community. The 2006 program was titled: "Shabbat, Sunday, and Jum'ah: Days of Meaning?" In 2009 our topic was: "What Do I Want the Other to Teach About My Religion?" and featured a minister, rabbi, and imam. We have also challenged ourselves with more sensitive material. At the 2013 Day of Dialogue, "Thin Places: Where We Touch Holiness," Dr. Peter A. Pettit, director of the Institute for Jewish-Christian Understanding, was the keynote speaker. He introduced the participants "to one of the holiest places in all the world: the city of Jerusalem, Yerushalayim, al-Quds." Three members of the community shared personal experiences of being in Jerusalem.

Participation in the program has consistently hovered around 100, with roughly a 60/40 balance of Christians and Jews. Muslim participation has been more difficult to cultivate, with the best success at the events hosted by the masjids. Through public advertising and personal contacts, individuals from Baha'i, Sikh, Lenni Lenape (a local American Nation), Buddhist, and other communities have been participants and dialogue facilitators.

One of the most popular segments of every Day of Dialogue program is table dialogue discussions. Participants are seated at round tables with a conscious effort to assign a mix of Jews, Christians, and Muslims to each table. Every table has a facilitator who has attended a preparatory session to be familiar with the topic as well as with dialogue-facilitation issues. The discussions center on the keynote presentation(s), responses of panelists, and often specific texts that have been prepared for the table dialogues. This is where the real Day of Dialogue happens, as participants interact with those of another religious tradition in a safe environment. Frequent attendee Mary Lou Hatcher said about the dialogue, "I am convinced that movements as big as 'World Peace' begin with the simple honest conversations we have with neighbors who are different from ourselves." Another long-time participant, Carol Closson, noted, "One of the most valuable components is the gathering of people of different faiths who talk to each other, not only about beliefs that are in common with each other, but also about their differences."

The program has benefitted from our conscious decision to hold it in a variety of locations—churches, masjids, and synagogues, as well as on the campus of Muhlenberg College. For many participants, this may be the first time they have visited the sacred space of another tradition. Informal tours, especially of sanctuaries, often take place.

An additional component has been added to the Day of Dialogue in the past two years to encourage more direct, personal interaction among the participants. While we are still perfecting the mechanics of "speed-faithing," it has proven to be a very popular innovation. Participants are asked to pair off; one year they sat in two rows opposite each other, the next year they stood in two circles facing each other. The leader has a list of prepared questions and, after reading the question, each member of the pair has about ninety seconds to give her/his answer to the partner. Then the leader tells one member of the couple to move one slot, a new question is asked, and the new partners give answers to each other. This encourages everyone to think about their views and to articulate them. Every participant has an equal opportunity to speak.

Each Day of Dialogue, from content to mechanics, is overseen by a committee with Christian, Jewish, and Muslim representatives meeting with Dr. Pettit, the director of the IJCU. Particularly as we discuss varying topics and try to choose among the shared, pressing issues of organized religious traditions in America, committee members have engaged in many lively, provocative, and open exchanges. Indeed, more than one member has commented that planning the Day of Dialogue provides at least as much insight and encounter as the event itself!

CHAPTER FOUR

Our God and Their God
A RELATIONAL THEOLOGY OF RELIGIOUS PLURALITY

J. Paul Rajashekar

This chapter is an attempt to articulate a relevant and responsible theology of religious plurality faithful to Christian convictions and accountable to neighbors of other religions in our midst. It draws on personal struggles, experiences of inter-religious encounter, stories, and anecdotes to explore a range of theological issues that Christians are often faced with in relating to people of other religions. In order to assist the reader with the flow of this chapter I have highlighted some questions or salient points in each section. Answers to some challenging questions I raise in the early part will become apparent as the chapter progresses. Readers are advised to read the entire chapter for my views on some theologically difficult questions. I must however caution that while I have tried to anticipate the kind of questions that readers may bring to this topic, not *all* questions can be *theologically resolved* but must be *dialogically explored* with people of other faiths. Some questions, needless to say, by their very nature will always remain unanswered or remain a mystery in this side of eternity! With that caveat, I invite you to grapple with me on two critical issues of our times that this chapter seeks to address: How do we make sense of the existence of multiple religious traditions in our midst? What does it mean to be a Christian living in the midst of people of other religious faiths in a pluralistic society?

Call to Prayer

I have wrestled with those questions most of my life. As one who grew up in a multi-religious India, I distinctly remember waking up early in the morning listening to the call to prayer from a nearby mosque. The melodious voice of the muezzin: *"Allahhu Akbar, Allahhu Akbar"* (God is Greater! God is Greater!) still rings in my ear whenever I think of my early years.

I often wondered whether that call to prayer at five in the morning was intended only to those who belonged to the Muslim faith or was it also a call to me to begin my day with prayer. Raised in a Christian home, it wasn't unusual that every day my family too began the day with Scripture reading and prayer. Most of my Hindu friends also would begin their day with ritual bathing and the recitation of the morning prayer (often the *Gayathri Mantra*). My friends and I belonged to different religious traditions (Hindu, Muslim, Christian, Jain, etc.) and we all knew of our religious differences. Often where we lived (the street or locality) indicated our religious identity. We nonetheless respected each other's faith convictions and were careful not to question each other's faith or religious practices. We walked to school together, played soccer together, studied together, watched movies together, visited homes, and sometimes ate in one another's homes. But there was one thing that we never did: We never prayed together! Loyalty to our own faith required that we distance ourselves from one another or segregate ourselves when we conversed with God. I never gave much thought to our divergent beliefs or spiritual practices and accepted them as facts that we must live with and not argue about.

It was much later in life as a seminarian that I began to grapple more seriously with issues raised in a multi-religious society. A course I took on Islam under Kenneth Cragg, a Christian scholar on Islam, sharpened my questions and deepened my understanding about prayer.[1] In multi-faith societies, people of different faiths share the same social and cultural space as they work together, socialize together, do business together, and engage with one another in various ways every day, but when it comes to prayer we retreat into our segregated sanctuaries—Christian in the church, Hindu in the temple, Muslim in the mosque, Jew in the synagogue, Sikh in the *gurdwara*, and so forth. It seems the farther we are into our religious sanctuaries, the farther we are from one another! Does God hear our prayers only in the privacy of our sanctuaries? This is the way most communities have practiced, preserved, and protected the

> We are prone to think that others pray to "their God" and we pray to "our God." Is this really true?
>
> What kind of God is our God who hears Christian prayers but pays no head to the prayers of others?
>
> How do we understand prayer in a pluralistic society?

---

1 Kenneth Cragg, *Alive to God: Muslim and Christian Prayers* (London, Oxford, 1970).

distinctiveness and sanctity of their respective religious traditions. But it may also prompt us to raise further questions.

Does a religiously plural society, which invariably demands mutual acquaintance of religious faiths, exclude mutual recognition before God or the transcendent reality? Is prayer deemed authentic only in segregated communities or sanctuaries of humankind? Can Christians and people of other faith convictions relate with one another only in our theological debates and social engagements and not in our religious yearnings? Is there nothing between us in our religious identities except our dialogues and debates, mutual antagonisms and hatred, shared animosities or activism? When we walk together with religious others can we also pray together?

Some Christian Responses

Christians who have thought about such questions may offer different answers. Some may say that we all worship different gods. Others may say that the Christian God is the only true God and all other gods are false and their worship is in vain. Still others may say that the gods of others are idols, human creations made out of wood or stone, quoting Isaiah 44. Some Christians would say that God hears prayers only when they are lifted up "in the name of Jesus." We are prone to think that others pray to "their gods" and we pray to "our God," Jesus Christ. Does God hear prayers only when they are addressed or postmarked in the name of Jesus Christ? What kind of God is a God who hears Christian prayers but pays no heed to prayers of others offered in their places of worship? Is this really true? The fact that people of different faiths live in our midst and they too pray to God may cause us to rethink our own understanding of God and God's relationship with people who do not profess to be Christians. Are prayers of others wasted efforts in seeking God?

In 1986, Pope John Paul II convened an inter-religious prayer meeting for peace in Assisi, Italy. The pope received a lot of flak for convening such a gathering. Some Christians thought that the head of the Roman Catholic Church was *de facto* granting legitimacy to the religious beliefs of others. The meeting for some seemed to lend credence to the idea of parity among various religions. Some Christians were really disturbed that the pope would even consider praying with the spiritual heads of other religions. The Roman Curia was in a quandary, and they came up with an explanation indicating that the religious leaders were "coming together to pray" but "they are not praying together." To avoid any misunderstanding, the religious leaders went into their own separate corners to offer their prayers for peace!

In religiously plural societies, inter-religious gatherings for prayer and special purposes are becoming fairly common. Inter-religious prayer meetings have been organized in special situations especially when communities are affected by calamities, such as after 9/11 in New York and the Sandy Hook Elementary School shootings in Connecticut. In April 2015, when riots took place on the streets of Baltimore as a result of the death of a twenty-five year old black man, the clergy of all denominations (rabbis, pastors, and imams) walked hand in hand to restore peace and order. In June 2015, we saw powerful inter-religious representation in the aftermath of the Charleston tragedy (which resulted in the fatal shooting of nine people engaged in a Bible study by a racially motivated Christian youth) and during the funeral service in Charleston, South Carolina, for the slain Pastor Clementa Pinckney (a graduate of a Lutheran seminary). Again in July 2015, when a Muslim young man killed five guardsmen and injured others in Chattanooga, Tennessee, both Muslims and Christians participated in the memorial service at a Baptist church. Such events are necessary not only to comfort and bring about healing in multi-faith communities but also to rebuild communities torn apart by racial or inter-religious tensions and conflicts. This volume contains a case study of an inter-religious prayer service to end world hunger held in Des Moines, Iowa. Although such services are few and infrequent in most communities, the fact that they do happen gives us occasion to raise questions for Christians about prayer in a pluralistic society.

> What images of God do you have when you pray?
>
> Are those images different from images of those praying who identify with another religion?
>
> Do you believe that we are all praying to the same God?

Is "Our" God Listening?

In leading adult forums at Lutheran congregations, I have met people asking the question whether God listens to the prayer of all people whether Christian or not. Someone once asked me the question, "How come Muslims are able to draw people to pray five times a day while we Christians have trouble getting people to come to church once a week?" Questions such as these arise when we become aware of the worship practices of other communities: What does it mean to be a community of prayer living in the midst of other communities of prayer?

Chaim Potok, a Jewish novelist, raises a similar question as he refers to a young Jewish rabbi travelling in Japan.[2] At a Buddhist shrine, the rabbi observes an old Japanese man, prayer book in hand, slowly swaying back and forth as he stood in prayer. The rabbi asked his Jewish companion, "Do you think our God is listening to him?" "I don't know. . . . I never thought of it," says the companion. "Neither did I until now, replies the rabbi. "If our God is not listening, why not? If God is listening, then well, what are we all about?" The rabbi's question is a profoundly important one: If God is not listening, why not? What kind of God do we understand God to be, that God would not listen to the ardent prayers of this Buddhist man?

> If God is listening to the prayers of others, what are we about?
>
> Do beliefs shape prayer or does prayer shape beliefs?
>
> To acknowledge that our faith is one among the many religious options may imply we are relativizing our own faith.

Put this way, our quest is intimately tied up with our beliefs and theological convictions. In the Christian tradition there is a Latin phrase, *lex orandi, lex credendi*, which means that the way we pray is what we believe. Their relationship is reciprocal; beliefs and worship are intertwined, but in practice it is often our beliefs that shape our prayer. It is our divergent beliefs that can and do hold us back from seeking God in unison.

The thought that God may hear the prayers of others who do not confess the name of Jesus may create some measure of anxiety or insecurity among certain Christians about the uniqueness of their faith in the midst of other faiths. The fear of compromising the unique claims of the Christian faith is genuinely real, and any acknowledgment of the prayers of others may imply undermining the validity of Christian claims or questioning our loyalty to them. While we recognize the fact of religious diversity in our midst, the thought that there are other belief systems alternative to our own, competing with ours, is deeply disturbing or unnerving to some. To acknowledge that our faith is one among the many religious options may imply that we are relativizing our own faith. Relativism is a worldview in which differences don't matter or in which one cannot see clearly enough to make a value judgment among different religious beliefs and practices. Some may legitimately fear that

---

2 Chaim Potok, *The Book of Lights* (New York: Fawcett Crest, 1981).

such a view leads to an undermining, if not outright denial of the uniqueness of salvation in Jesus Christ and the biblical mandate to mission and evangelism.

In the face of such anxieties, Christians may want to hold tenaciously to their faith, choosing to ignore the presence of other faiths in our midst. Such a stance would imply a "cocoon mentality" by deliberately withholding engagement with others or by adopting an indifferent view toward others. Exposure to and awareness of pluralism can make us all turn inward and steadfastly hold on to the security of our own faith. The rise of religious "fundamentalism" among many religious communities today is ironically correlated to exposure to pluralism in our world.

Another alternative is vehemently to deny, confront, or repudiate the validity of other religious claims. Such a stance is often fueled by contemporary events and the headline news about religion-inspired violence, hatred, destruction of places of worship, persecution of religious minorities, terrorism, and beheading of innocent people by extremist groups in our world. Understandably, our fears are exacerbated, our prejudices confirmed, and we are prone to develop an attitude of intolerance towards people who engage in inhumane behaviors in the name of their religion. The temptation therefore is to vilify, stereotype, or caricature others and their beliefs. It is also a human temptation to put the best construction on the values of one's own faith and put the worst construction on the values of others!

When I began writing these reflections, the public buses in Philadelphia, Pennsylvania, were carrying an advertisement promoting religious hatred against Muslims as a matter of free political speech. The advertisement was sponsored by a New Hampshire-based group, the American Freedom Defense Initiative, primarily targeting Muslims but also affecting Jews, Sikhs, and others wearing visible religious garb. It won a court case against the objections of the local transportation authority. Civil and religious leaders in the area issued a statement condemning the advertisements for derogatory and hurtful speech. Western societies today are engaged in a fierce debate about the limits to free speech vs. respect for the sentiments of religious communities.

Most Christians do not harbor overt hostility or engage in hate speech toward people of other faiths, but they are nonetheless sensitive to, or suspicious of, the presence of other religious faiths in their community. Fear or unfamiliarity of the other are often the cause of communal tensions. There is a long simmering controversy in Hamtramck, a small town outside of Detroit, over public prayers. The main mosque in the town began broadcasting—over loudspeakers—the Muslim call to prayer five times a day approved by the city council. Predictably, some residents felt uncomfortable to hear the call to prayer coming from a mosque. "They have crossed the line," said some. "It's no different from tolling of the church bells," said others. A longtime resident stated the issue thus: "I used to say that I wasn't prejudiced against anyone, but then I realized I had a problem with them [Muslims] putting Allah above everything else." For the last few years the residents of Hamtramck are grappling with issues of religious freedom and what it means to live in a multi-faith community.[3]

Coming to terms with religious plurality is not about denying or harmonizing religious differences among people. Differences can be seen either as a threat or a source of mutual enrichment to one's faith. Cultural or racial prejudice, political or ethnic conflicts, and the fear of the other play a major role in perceiving religious differences as a threat to our self-identity. Where there are no established relationships or trust among communities, religious differences often get exaggerated or heightened. It is important to recognize that differences do not diminish but rather enlarge the sphere of human possibilities. Religious differences in community therefore need not be feared, for they implicitly or explicitly invite us to engage with others who differ from us. This engagement is much harder to do if there are no healthy relationships between communities. To engage in dialogue requires commitment to one's own faith and openness toward others. *The burden of an interfaith society therefore is precisely the meaning of our faith in the midst of other faiths.* Only when we are willing to recognize differences in faith communities—not wishing everyone be the same—are we able to establish a *bona fide* (good faith) relationship with all people in community.

> Religious differences can be seen either as a threat or a source of enrichment to one's faith.
>
> Inter-religious dialogue is primarily between people and not between religions.
>
> The behavior of some believers does not necessarily represent the beliefs and values of their respective faiths.

This look at the idea of engaging one another leads me to make an obvious point: *Inter-religious dialogue and engagement is primarily be-*

---

3 http://www.nytimes.com/2004/05/05/us/tension-in-a-michigan-city-over-muslims-call-to-prayer. html?_r = 0. Elizabeth Hayes Alvarez, "Neighbors, Fences and Religion in America," *Sightings*, Martin E. Marty Center at The University of Chicago, May 27, 2004 (electronic edition).

tween people who embody different faiths and not between the doctrinal beliefs to which they subscribe. Doctrines and beliefs allow us to understand, define, and interpret our world and human existence in a rational way, or at least, in a way that makes the world sensible and approachable. Christians tend to place a greater emphasis on beliefs/doctrines in defining themselves whereas most other faiths emphasize religious practice rather than beliefs/doctrines. Beliefs/doctrines, as we all know, vary between different faiths and often among those who share the same faith or religious tradition. Religions of the world offer alternate visions of the human situation and ways of life leading to the ultimate destiny of humans and the created order. Dialogues between such alternate visions or doctrinal beliefs are helpful and necessary in promoting mutual understanding and cooperation, but how people practice and express their faith in daily life is what matters most in society rather than the beliefs they adhere to.

What is paramount is how people practice and embody their faith and confession, that is, how they experience and express the reality of the divine or divine grace in their lives; how they attend to prayer, worship, and interpersonal relationships; what life-affirming values and habits they hold; their commitment to justice and human dignity; how they accept and care for their neighbors; how they serve to build community; and so forth. We must recognize that beliefs and practices are very much intertwined and yet there is always a gap between our precepts and our practices, our beliefs and our behavior. It should be obvious therefore that the behavior of some believers does not necessarily represent the beliefs and values of their respective faiths. Inter-religious engagement therefore is not primarily about comparing religions or doctrines (though such endeavors help to build theological bridges between religious communities) but rather is about an encounter between committed people who follow different religious convictions. At the level of human mutuality we are able to understand, discern, relate, and even appreciate differences in our religious perspectives.

"Let Everything That Breathes Praise the LORD"

It hardly needs to be said that Christians do not have a monopoly on the holy. We recognize this in our indebtedness to Judaism. We, in fact, have borrowed prayers from that tradition. In our communal worship we frequently use the Jewish psalter, and together with Jews we sing praises to the Lord. There are indeed differences and disagreements between

Jews and Christians and divergent appropriation of a shared scriptural tradition. Nonetheless, Christians have been doggedly loyal to the Hebrew Scriptures, notwithstanding Marcion (a second century Christian who rejected the value of Hebrew Scriptures for Christians). The Hebrew psalmody is undeniably a source of spiritual enrichment for Christians of all ages. Together with Jews we have unreservedly affirmed the call to pray found in Psalm 150:6: "Let everything that breathes praise the LORD" (NRSV). We have also found resonance with Psalm 148 in its call of both the animal and natural world to praise the Lord.

In doing so we acknowledge that like breath, prayer is a human need, an expression of our finitude, a search for relationship with the One who is beyond us all. Because we human beings are creatures who are mere mortals, must suffer, are ignorant, and in pain, everywhere human beings have reached out to a transcendent Other that might help them out of their mortality, redeem them from their suffering, enlighten their ignorance, heal their pain, grant them forgiveness, or liberate them from their bondage. No doubt, as humans we pray out of obedience, habit, or desire. But fundamentally prayer is a common act to reach out beyond ourselves. From the standpoint of a Christian theology of creation, there is nothing peculiar or significant about Christian prayer in comparison with Muslim, Hindu, Buddhist, or any other religious tradition. In the book of Malachi, the Lord God says, "For from the rising of the sun to its setting my name is great among the nations, and in every place incense is offered to my name, and a pure offering; for my name is great among nations, says the LORD of Hosts." (1:11, NRSV).

> Does the authenticity of prayer depend on confessional correctness?
>
> Are prayers deemed authentic only when addressed "in the name of Jesus Christ"?
>
> Western Christians may have grudgingly yielded some cultural and social space for people of other faiths in society in recent decades, but are we prepared to yield a "theological space" for others to flourish?

I have often wrestled with the question: If prayer is a human response to God, then aren't all prayers offered by people, irrespective of their faith convictions, legitimate responses to God? Are their responses to God whether in prayer or in their articulation of religious beliefs any less legitimate than our own? On many occasions I have had opportunities to observe the prayers of Muslims at the mosque, Hindus in the temple, Jews at the synagogue, Sikhs in the *gurdwara*, and Buddhists in their shrines. Listening to their prayers, I was hardly surprised to hear words, sentiments, supplications, and resonances similar to my own. I couldn't help but acknowledge the genuineness or sincerity of their prayers notwithstanding the fact that their responses to God are based on different beliefs and creeds. And yet, the authenticity and propriety of prayers of others is something we Christians ought not to doubt or question, and they may even prompt us to rethink our understanding of God's compassion for all people. Would "our" God hear the prayers of others whose beliefs are rooted in other religious convictions which are incompatible with our own? Are prayers deemed authentic and proper only if they are rooted in creedal correctness?

Prayers of people of other faiths, as someone would surely point out, are addressed to "their Gods." This is an important question. Prayers of most faiths contain an "implicit or explicit referent": the "object" of praise, adoration or supplication, without which prayers become empty words. But we must pursue the question further: Are we to suppose God is heedless unless "God" is properly addressed and understood, or that our prayers must always conform to the doctrinal prescriptions of our religious tradition? Put differently, does doctrinal correctness dictate or determine formulations of prayer or, conversely, does the rule of prayer precede the rule of belief? In a real sense, private and personal prayers and supplications are beyond external scrutiny. It is hardly conceivable today that divine compassion is dependent on doctrinal purity or theological correctness. As the letter of Hebrews has it, "Whoever would approach him [God] must believe that he exists and he rewards those who seek him" (11:6, NRSV). I shall return to these questions later on.

> We know our faith from the inside and all others from the outside. It is unavoidable that we tend to define and interpret others in our own terms, our framework of understanding according to our doctrinal beliefs, and pre-suppositions, and not in terms of other's self-definitions.

Our discussion thus far on prayer in relation to faith and beliefs of others may push us to rethink the depth and riches of God's love and mercy for all people. It is evident that Western societies have made some strides, albeit grudgingly, to provide some *social and cultural space* to people whose beliefs and practices differ from our own. But as Christians we have difficulty in according a *theological space* for people of other faiths, that is, a theological recognition of the legitimacy of their religious claims.

This problem is not an exclusively Christian one; it is a problem for most religious faiths living in multi-religious societies. It is, however, felt far more keenly by Christian and Muslim traditions than others. It is obvious that religious faiths by their very nature tend to be particular. They are rooted in a particular context, culture, or history and expect allegiance to beliefs, doctrines, values, and ritual traditions from their adherents. Claims of particular identity, chosen-ness or uniqueness are therefore woven into the doctrinal fabric of most faiths. This fact by and large explains differences in religious worldviews. That said, we know our faith from the inside and all others from the outside. It is therefore unavoidable that we tend to define and interpret others in our own terms, our framework of understanding, doctrinal beliefs, and presuppositions, and not in terms of others' self-definitions. We look at the world wearing our own religious and cultural lenses. We are, therefore, prone to define others in negative terms, such as "non-Christians" or "non-Lutherans," rather than in positive terms according to their self-chosen identity. It is a temptation to put the best construction on our beliefs and claims and the worst construction on the beliefs and claims of others! Religious differences, cultural conflicts, and historical antagonisms among religions therefore have prevented mutual cognizance or acknowledgement of one another. *Our inherited theologies, prejudices, and claims of religious particularity have not been readily open to providing a theological space for us to engage in a positive, honest and bona fide relationship with neighbors of other faiths.* This is our present burden and task that we must pursue today. That is, to articulate a relevant and responsible *theology of religious plurality* faithful to our convictions and accountable to our neighbors.

Our God, Their God

While Christians are willing to recognize that God is the creator of all people, some are hesitant to acknowledge that God is responsive to the prayers of others. As noted earlier, some are of the conviction that prayers of others are addressed to "their Gods." We have occasionally heard some Christian leaders pronounce that the Muslim Allah is different from the Christian God. Despite a shared Abrahamic ancestry and a shared commitment to monotheism among Jews, Christians, and Muslims, somehow there is a perception among some Christians that Muslims and Christians worship different Gods. We even forget that Arabic-speaking Christians in the Middle East and Christians in Malaysia and Indonesia use the word "Allah" to refer to God. The fact that the so-called Abrahamic religions profess a "monotheistic" belief, implying that they believe in "one" God, may require a closer examination. The Jewish creed, the *Shema*, proclaims, "Hear, O Israel: The LORD our God is one Lord" (Deuteronomy 6:4 KJV) is echoed in the Muslim *Shahadah* (creed), "There is no god save God. . . ." The intent of these creedal statements is to affirm that the Ultimate Reality is one and not many. Islam in particular is insistent that the word "God" (Allah) is incapable of being made plural, "Say: He is God, the One" (Sura 112:1). To believe otherwise is to subscribe to a "polytheistic" (that there are many gods) view.

Both Christianity and Islam are indebted to a Jewish understanding of God. In the Hebrew Bible, there are two streams of thought evident. First, there is the notion that there are "true God" and "false gods" displayed in the strong prophetic criticism of idols and idol worship and in the attempts (as in the story of Elijah and the prophets of Baal, 1 Kings 18: 24-25) to prove that Yahweh is more powerful than other gods worshipped by nations surrounding Israel. Second, there is the belief that Yahweh is the "God of the nations." Israelites were faced with a clear choice: Either they had to admit that Yahweh (their Lord) is their "tribal god," one among the many gods, or that Yahweh is God over all nations and people. The complex developments in the evolution of the Israelite understanding of God ultimately led to the belief that is best captured in the opening verses of Psalm 24: "The earth is the LORD's and all that is in it, the world, and those who live in it."

> It is a central affirmation of the Christian faith that God is One.
>
> To believe otherwise is to subscribe to an unacknowledged "polytheism."
>
> There is only One God, but there are indeed different perceptions or models of understanding God in religious communities.

The sovereignty and oneness of God is a foundational belief among Jews, Christians, and Muslims, although Christians affirm the oneness of God in trinitarian terms. Christians who think otherwise may learn from St. Paul's advice to the Corinthian Christians that "no idol in the world really exists, and that there is *no God but one*" (1 Corinthians 8:4,NRSV, emphasis added). St. Paul goes on to say, "Indeed, even though there may be so-called gods in heaven or on earth—as in fact there are many gods and many lords—yet for us there is one God, the Father, from whom all things and for whom we exist, and one Lord Jesus Christ, through whom are all things and through whom we exist" (1 Corinthians 8:5-6, NRSV).

In light of St. Paul's admonition, we Christians must be cautious about our pronouncements and judgments about the beliefs of other people or their perceptions about God. To think that there are many gods goes against our monotheistic conviction and thereby subscribes to an "unacknowledged polytheism." This is not to deny, however, that although there is only one God, there are indeed different perceptions, images, and understandings of God. Religious traditions through the ages have offered different or divergent articulations of the meaning of God within their own theological/religious/cultural frameworks. The Muslim tradition thus speaks of God in terms of ninety-nine names. The *Upanishads* in the Hindu tradition speaks of *Brahman* (the Ultimate Reality), both in terms of having no attributes (*nirguna*) and with specific attributes (*saguna*). Buddhism, on the other hand, chooses to refrain from any form of speculation about God or the Ultimate Reality.

Christians do not often realize that God is a symbol in so far as the term points to a reality that cannot be fully described or grasped. Several religious traditions, including a variety of Christian thinkers over the centuries, therefore employ the method of "negative theology," that is, describing God in terms of what "God is not" rather than what "God is." Speaking of the indescribable aspect of the Ultimate Reality, the Hindu mystic Thirumooler observed, "Those that have experienced it can never describe it; those who describe it never experience it!"[4] Though this may be an over-statement, the intent is to caution us against absolutizing any statements about God or the Ultimate Reality.

The foregoing discussion leads us to a central affirmation of the Christian faith that God is one. Two corollary affirmations follow: 1) It would be contrary to our monotheistic perception of God to think that there can be a Muslim God, a Christian God, and Hindu gods. It is the one God that we Christians affirm (albeit understood in trinitarian terms) who is the same God, who is the creator and provider of the universe, who is in relationship with people of all religious beliefs and traditions. That is part of our theology of creation. It shouldn't be surprising or shocking therefore to acknowledge that God indeed hears the prayers of all people, irrespective of religious commitments. 2) Though there is only one God, there are indeed different models of understanding or divergent perceptions and descriptions of God. The oneness of God or the Ultimate Reality is something most religious faiths share. But it is our

---

4 Cited by Wesley Ariarajah, *Your God, My God and Our God: Rethinking Christian Theology for Religious Plurality* (Geneva: World Council of Churches, 2012).

differences in beliefs and our theological/religious responses to the One that invite mutual dialogue and explorations.

Are All Religions the Same?

My reflections thus far may have provoked anxiety or uncertainty in the minds of some readers. The affirmation of the oneness of God and God's relationship with people of other faiths could be interpreted to mean all religions are the same or that it makes no difference whether one is a Christian, Muslim, Hindu, or Buddhist. There are many who think that all religions are the same and their differences more a matter of varied colors than of conflicting content. They adopt a theology of neutrality that treats all religions as equally valid and true. Some have used the analogy that religions are different paths to climb the same mountain. It is important therefore to be clear about what I mean by "religion" and to dispel some common misconceptions about inter-religious engagement.

In simple terms, religion is a view of life and a way of life. Different religions offer different views of life and prescribe divergent paths to attain the ultimate end in life. There is a bewildering variety of religions in our world, and Christians therefore need to be judicious to discern what constitutes a legitimate religion or religious path. The task is not always easy when individuals and groups mask their ideologies under the guise of religion! Here I am primarily concerned with religions that have attained historical legitimacy as "world religions." Anyone acquainted with a faint knowledge of living religions of the world would readily acknowledge that these religions or religious traditions, notwithstanding certain commonalities, offer divergent visions of life and ways of living it. One cannot, therefore, ignore or reduce profound differences among religious traditions. It is erroneous to believe that all religions are the same. Not all religious paths lead to the same mountaintop. Perhaps, they lead to different mountaintops!

That said, difference doesn't imply right or wrong, true or false convictions. Acknowledging differences implies neither acceptance nor denial. Rather, difference invites us to dialogue, conversation, exploration, and mutual understanding. We are often right in what we affirm, but we are more often wrong in what we deny. What we affirm is something that we are intimately familiar with, but what we deny often something that we know or understand the least. When we deny others, we are subject to denial by others. Christians therefore need to be cautious in denying or rejecting the religious claims of others. Discerning the authentic from the bogus, the divine from the demonic, the good from the evil, in various religious expressions is not easy. Our judgments about the authenticity of others therefore require patient hearing and understanding.

> It is erroneous to hold the view that all religions are the same. Not all religious paths lead to the same mountain top.
>
> Religious differences do not imply right or wrong, true or false convictions.
>
> We are often right in what we affirm, but we are more often wrong in what we deny.
>
> Christians should be wary of false characterization of beliefs and practices of others.

I came to realize this fact early in life. I was often appalled to see Hindu gods and goddesses portrayed in the form of idols with multiple hands, eyes, and heads in temples and in pictorial representations. Not only do they look grotesque, but it also seemed absurd to me to worship and venerate deities made out of stone or metal. I often thought of Hindus as idol worshippers, until I met a Hindu scholar who taught me that God is "formless" and genderless but we humans require "forms," "images," and "symbols" as instruments to imagine and conceptualize God. It is not that Hindus worship idols, for they know that idols are human creations, but idols point to a reality that is beyond human grasp. Hindu gods and goddesses are therefore portrayed with multiple hands, heads, and eyes in order to remind of the omnipotence, omnipresence, and omniscience of God. The Hindu scholar chided me by saying, "Do you think we are stupid to worship idols made out of wood and stone? We know where these idols came from and who crafted them. The Hindu tradition has long reflected about the meaning of idol worship and written voluminous treatises about it centuries ago." Little did I know the depth of Hindu reflections of God and their approaches to God. I was wrong in assuming or imposing Jewish/Christian/Islamic prejudice toward any forms of idolatry upon Hindus.

Upon further reflection, I came to the realization that humans do need finite objects, images, or even doctrines that help our understanding of God and God's presence among us, whether in the form of the cross, icons, stained glass windows, painted portraits of Jesus in our homes, the bread and wine at the altar, creeds and confessions, and so forth. Humans therefore are not totally free from focusing on objects as we worship or pray. We invariably have the tendency and the need to imagine or formulate our perception of God in some concrete ways.

When Martin Luther, while exiled in the Wartburg Castle, heard that the people in Wittenberg were destroying religious statues and breaking stained-glass windows, he dressed as a knight and traveled to Wittenberg to object. He preached eight sermons on the subject of religious practices and Christian freedom. So long as portraits and symbols are not the object of worship, he said, they can be aids to worship. Because Christians also use aids to worship, it is a false caricature of other religions to assume that the aids they use—even though unfamiliar to us—are idols. On the other hand, as Luther points out in his Large Catechism, regarding anything other than God to be of ultimate importance in life, whether that "other" is material, mental, or conceptual, is to make it our god and therefore our idol. This may occur in any religion, Christianity included.

> Humans are not totally free from focusing on objects and images as we worship and pray.
>
> When we elevate anything other than God to be of ultimate importance in life, we make it our idol.
>
> Martin Luther

The fact that religious faiths have differing perceptions of God, human existence, and the ultimate goal of life need not withhold us from engaging with others. People of other faiths have similar fears, reservations, and apprehensions about relating with us Christians! In the course of history, Christian interaction with people of other faiths has been by and large more negative than positive. Memories of such interactions (sometimes violent!) arouse genuine fears in the minds of others when Christian overtures of dialogue and hospitality in today's world are viewed as another ploy to convert them to the Christian faith. Others have been the targets of our evangelism and mission rather than being received as partners in community, fellow citizens in religious or spiritual pilgrimage in their own way. While Christians profess to love our neighbors, we have miserably fallen short in practice. A professor of mine often reminded us that "2000 years of Christian love makes anyone nervous!" Overcoming the burdens and failure of our past interactions and continued antagonism demands that we strive to articulate a *new relationship* or a new understanding of a theology of hospitality. Adopting such a posture of mutual acknowledgment ought not to minimize profound differences between religious faiths nor maximize mutual tensions and antagonism by comparing the best of our own faith with the worst of others. I will have more to say about inter-religious hospitality later on.

Christ Among Religions

Granted, there are profound differences and disagreements between religious faiths that warrant mutual understanding and dialogue, but there is still the question of Jesus Christ in relation to other religions. Thoughtful readers may ask: It is one thing to affirm the oneness of God as the sovereign Lord of all creation, but it is another thing to place Jesus alongside other saviors, prophets, religious teachers, or spiritual leaders. Are we relativizing the unique revelation of God in Jesus Christ for the sake of inter-religious cooperation and understanding? In other words, are we not undermining the heart of Christian identity in the interest of external relations?

Questions such as these invariably arise in inter-religious situations leading to passionate arguments among Christians. The fear of surrendering the distinctiveness of Jesus as the Christ or Jesus as God may prompt Christians to pause in their engagement with people of other faiths. Christian theologians have called this the "christological problem" in inter-religious relations. The "problem" can neither be avoided nor evaded, and we ought to address it with all honesty and sincerity. Among the three articles of the Christian creeds (the Apostles' Creed and the Nicene Creed) the substantial portion of the creeds is about Jesus, his birth, death, and resurrection. Without the affirmation that *Jesus is the Christ of God*, Christian faith has no meaning or relevance in a pluralistic society.

How Jesus Christ is related to those who profess other faiths is a question with which I continue to grapple. Similar to Pastor Nelson in Chapter Three, early in my pastoral ministry, my wife (who is also a Lutheran pastor) and I were engaged in Lutheran Hour radio ministry in our mother tongue (Kannada) in South India. It was not a program of explicit evangelism but a broad discussion of the meaning of Christian faith illustrated in stories, life experiences, music, and drama. This program received such a tremendous response (some five to seven thousand letters per week!) that we were not prepared nor did we have the resources to respond to them all. In reading through the letters we

> Are we relativizing the unique revelation of God in Jesus Christ for sake of interreligious cooperation?

> Christian encounters with others in history by and large have been negative and hostile.

> How is Christ related to those other claims to religious truth and experiences of divine grace?

received, we were astonished to find that 80 percent of our listeners were Hindus! Even more surprising to us was that the letters contained moving testimonies, poetry, stories, healing and spiritual experiences acknowledging Jesus Christ as their Lord and Savior or a profound admiration for the life and teachings of Jesus Christ. What was disturbing in those letters was that a vast majority of those who professed Jesus as their Savior expressed no desire to be baptized or associate themselves with the Christian church!

We were baffled by the sheer number of people who had no hesitation to confess their faith in Jesus Christ but were reluctant to be associated with the Christian church. The history of Western colonialism and aggressive Christian proselytism may have been factors in their rejection of the church as a Western implant in a predominantly Hindu India. But at a much deeper level, responses to radio broadcasts raised some profound questions.

How is Jesus Christ related to those people of other religions? Is Christ a savior only to those who publicly confess Jesus and are baptized? In other words, is Christ a Christian "tribal god" and therefore unrelated to neighbors of other faiths? How do we understand the existence of millions of people in Asia and elsewhere who implicitly or explicitly profess to follow Christ and yet choose to remain as unbaptized believers or anonymous Christians? (in contrast to many baptized unbelievers in Western societies)? Is Christ present in the beliefs and spiritualties of others unknown to them? Is explicit confession of Christ a prerequisite for salvation even though in Christian conviction Christ died for redemption of *all* people?

Questions such as these are not entirely new in a multi-faith context. Christian faith itself emerged in a multi-religious context. Early Christian theologians, church fathers—even the Apostle Paul—did wrestle with such questions. St. Paul spoke about the "unknown god" (Acts 17:23) as a way to relate with the Athenians. Some church fathers, like Justin Martyr (a second century Christian apologist), attempted to relate Christian faith through the use of the Greek concept of *logos* (the divine Word found in John 1:1) although based on the assumption of the superiority of Christian revelation over pagan religions and philosophies. Tertullian (also a second century church father), on the other hand, was vehemently opposed to such efforts by arguing, "What has Jerusalem got to do with Athens?" As a result, Christian relations with other religious faiths remained an ongoing issue in much of Christian history, notwithstanding the fact that the Christian faith was considerably enriched by pagan (Greek) philosophies and religious thought in its doctrinal formulations.

Medieval and Reformation theologians, living as they were in a predominantly mono-religious and culturally circumscribed context of the "Christendom" in Europe, were unable to overcome their historical prejudices and hostility toward Jews and Muslims. For much of Christian history Christians were antagonistic towards Jews and at war with Muslims. Medieval theologians, monks, and scholars with rare exceptions (like Francis of Assisi) were unable to overcome their historically inherited prejudices against other religious faiths. It is well known that Martin Luther wrote harsh and negative treatises against Jews. Lutherans today have distanced themselves from such derogatory views. What is less known, however, is that Luther also wrote six treatises on Islam comparing the Turkish religion (Islam) and the Christian religion, Christ and Prophet Muhammad. Despite his negative and derogatory assessment of Islam, Luther was instrumental in publishing the Latin version of the Qur'an and wrote a preface to it in 1542.[5] Luther never met a Muslim and may have met a few Jews, but his apologetic intent prejudiced his views of others. He genuinely feared that someday Saxony might come under the rule of Muslim Turks, and so he wanted to prepare his fellow Christians to live under a Muslim ruler.

Until the dawn of the modern era European Christians had few opportunities to interact with people of other faiths, and their knowledge of other faiths was limited. The theologies that emerged in the period of the Reformation therefore tended to be negative, if not hostile, toward people of other religions based on ignorance and cultural prejudice. This European prejudice was carried into other continents and cultures during the era of European geographical conquest and mercantile expansion from the fifteenth century onwards and into the era of modern Christian missions in Asia, Africa, and the Americas under colonial patronage. Christ was often understood as standing in judgment against other non-Western (or non-European) cultures and religions. Christian theologies developed in the West thus continue to maintain notions of religious and cultural superiority and a negative view of other religions. This in part explains why other cultures and religions to this day continue to harbor resentment toward the Christian faith and its claims.

---

5 See J. Paul Rajashekar, "Luther and Islam: An Asian Perspective," *Lutherjahrbuch* (1990): 57:174-91; J. Paul Rajashekar and Timothy Wengert, "Martin Luther, Philip Melanchthon and the Publication of the Qur'an," *Lutheran Quarterly* (2002): 16:221-228.

But in light of the contemporary resurgence of other religious traditions in our world and globalization of religions, exclusive claims of Christian religious superiority have become not only problematic but also vigorously contested by others. The reality of religious pluralism in our world has shaken the confidence of assumed superiority of Christian faith over against other faiths. The Christian faith has long struggled to overcome the division between master and slave (racism), male and female (gender bias), Jews and Gentiles (cf. Galatians 3:28). In St. Paul's context, the "gentiles" were those not ethnically Jewish, and Paul urged his fellow Jewish believers to embrace unconditionally gentiles of Greco-Roman heritage. Today however we need to ask the question: Whom do we consider as the "gentiles" in our society? Are they the people of another race, ethnicity, language, or religious tradition different from our own? We can no longer avoid the question of the relationship between Christians and religious others. That question has now acquired greater intensity than in previous eras of Christian history.

> Who are the "gentiles" in our society?
>
> The challenge of religious pluralism can neither be wished away, nor can we insist on the superiority of Christian claims over against other counter-claims.

In an age of religious pluralism and the globalization of religions, Christians cannot assume that their religious claims will sway the world. Despite the phenomenal growth of Christianity in the southern hemisphere in recent decades, two-thirds of the world's population adheres to other beliefs or no belief. If we are honest, we must admit that all Christian efforts to engage in global mission are unlikely to alter that demographic reality. Today, the notion of "global mission" has been met with considerable resistance from other religions. In the minds of many, "global mission" carries with it the connotation of Christian conquest or world domination, reminiscent of the colonial era. Not only does the notion appear presumptuous, it is also deemed offensive, for it undermines the individual and communal rights of others to profess and practice their own inherited beliefs. Such fears have prompted some non-Western societies to promulgate anti-conversion laws or impose stringent restrictions on religious conversions. Those of us who live in North America should therefore understand the religious sensitivities of others in matters of conversion, and we must come to terms with the fact that religious pluralism in our midst is here to stay. Put differently, the challenge of religious pluralism can neither be wished away nor can we continue to insist on the superiority of Christian claims over against counterclaims by doubling up on our mission activities. We are thus compelled to articulate anew the meaning of Christian distinctiveness without denigrating other faiths in a globalized world. Religious plurality in society invariably relativizes all faiths. That the Christian faith is one among many religious options in the world whether we Christians like it or not!

Such a forthright acknowledgement of our religious reality is by no means a denial of the distinctiveness of the Christian faith. As Christians we are indeed truthful to insist on the *distinctiveness* of God's revelation in Jesus Christ; that is, in Christian understanding God has revealed Godself "once and for all" and demonstrated God's love and mercy for all humanity in the cross and resurrection of Jesus. However, our articulations of this belief have not fully explored the *relational distinctiveness* of Jesus Christ in the midst of other faiths. It is *relational* because, I believe, Christ does not remain unrelated to people of all faiths whether they acknowledge his saving work or not. It is the Christian claim that Christ died for *all* people. And yet, we are not sure how the saving work of Christ is related to people who profess alternate responses to the mystery and oneness of God. *How is Christ related to those other claims to religious truth and experiences of divine grace? Is it possible to affirm the distinctiveness of God's revelation in Christ while at the same time articulating a relational understanding of Christ?*

Bible and Other Faiths

Before I proceed to explore a relational understanding of Christ, it may be necessary to pause and address briefly the issue of scripture in relation to other faiths. Claims of Christian uniqueness are invariably based on biblical assertions or authority. There is a vast array of biblical materials, both in the Hebrew Scriptures and the New Testament, that address the issue of relations with people of other faiths. Among the many New Testament passages, Christians are prone to focus primarily on selected passages, such as John 14:6 and Acts 4:12,

Biblical texts are not intended to be read as texts of comparative religion.

John 14:6 in its context is about following "the way of the cross" as "the truth and the life."

Jesus indeed defines the meaning of God for Christians, but Jesus does not confine God.

In a multi-scriptural society, quoting scriptural texts does not resolve contesting claims to truth.

texts that make exclusive claims about Jesus Christ. There are many others: 1 Corinthians 3:11, 1 Timothy 2:5, Romans 1:21, John 3:36, and 1 John 5:12. How do we interpret such passages? Reading them in their context would indicate that they were *not* intended to be texts of comparative religion although Christians tend to use them that way. I will explore here only two crucial texts.[6]

Jesus' response to Thomas—"I am the way, the truth and the life. No one comes to the Father except through me" (John 14:6)—is set in the context of his impending entry to Jerusalem, anticipating his death on the cross. Jesus in his farewell discourses is urging his disciples to follow *his* way, the "way of the cross" as "the truth and the life" for his disciples. It is through suffering and death on the cross, through humility and vulnerability of discipleship, that his followers will have access to God the Father. To be a disciple means to adopt a "crucified mind" rather than a "crusading spirit." A "crucified mind" embraces people without pre-condition or reservation in contrast to the "crusading spirit" that seeks to conquer and subjugate the other. The cross of Jesus therefore is not a symbol of triumphalism or subjugation of people to Christ's lordship, but rather a symbol of God's relatedness and participation in the life and sufferings of *all God's people,* not just of Christians.

The Lutheran tradition therefore has long emphasized the *theology of the cross* as the central theme of the Christian faith. It is in the cross of Christ that "God in Christ" demonstrates God's relatedness and love for all people and offers unmerited grace, irrespective of their religious affiliation or commitments. Christ therefore is not unrelated to people of other faiths, whether they are explicitly aware of this truth or acknowledge it or not. Yet, even without awareness or explicit acknowledgment, people can indeed come to know God through an encounter with God's overflowing love and mercy, whether or not this encounter is tied to the name of Jesus. This is a central Christian conviction.

What appears as a text of Christian exclusivism in John 14:6, when read in the context of Jesus' farewell discourses to his disciples, is really a call to *practice the theology of the cross* as the way to God the Father. The focus of that text is about Christian discipleship, that is, following the way of the cross as life-giving truth. The text attests to the Christian conviction that in the event of the cross God discloses and defines the meaning of divine compassion for all people. Therefore God's love in

---

6 For an exploration on how the Bible views other religions, see S. Wesley Ariarajah, *Bible and People of Other Faiths* (Geneva: World Council of Churches, 1985).

Jesus Christ is not an exclusive possession of Christians. Jesus indeed *defines* the meaning of God for Christians, but Jesus does not *confine* God or limit God's boundless love. Christians therefore dare not put limits on the availability of God's amazing grace and compassion towards all people. It is in this spirit we read such texts as John 3:16, NRSV ("God so loved the world"), Philippians. 2:4-8, NRSV (Christ "emptied himself taking the form of slave."), and John 1:14, NRSV ("The Word became flesh and lived among us.").

Similarly, consider Peter's confession before the religious authorities in Acts 4:12, NRSV, "There is salvation in no one else, for there is no other name under heaven given among mortals by which we must be saved." The context of the confession was the *healing* of a crippled beggar (Acts 3), and the healing took place in the "name" of Jesus and "no other name." It was a statement of fact, a profound testimony to the healing power of God in Jesus Christ, an extension of Jesus' earthly ministry. Christians thus should avoid the temptation of taking Peter's confession out of context and universalizing it as a judgment against other names, other saviors, or other religious paths. To do so is to misuse Scripture. Proclaiming Jesus as the unique Son of God or Savior by early Christians was intended to say something positive about Jesus; it was not meant to say something negative about Buddha or any other name.

The so-called "exclusive" texts when read out of context as universal statements can indeed hold us back in exploring good-faith relationships with neighbors of other faiths. It is hard for us to resist the temptation of citing Scripture, as if that settles or resolves the issue. The authority of the Bible is indeed important to Christians. But Christians are prone to ignore the fact that in multi-religious societies there are other scriptures whose authority serves as the basis for the claims of others. If Christians cite their scriptures, others too can cite theirs! Hurling scriptural texts against one another does not resolve contesting claims to truth and revelation in society. Today most societies are multi-scriptural,

> The incarnation of the divine in the person of Jesus Christ is intrinsically an act of salvation.
>
> In the event of the cross, the passion history of Jesus enters into the passion history of all humanity.
>
> The religious histories of people cannot remain unaffected by the history of Jesus.

meaning no one scriptural tradition functions as the norm for all. Especially in Western societies it is often assumed that the Bible and Christian values serve as the foundation for governing society, disregarding the presence of other scriptural traditions and values. As religious pluralism becomes more and more pronounced in Western societies, *all religious faiths* must come to terms with the reality of one another's scriptures. In multi-faith societies religious claims based on one scriptural tradition have no more validity or privileged status than the claims based on other scriptural traditions. Pluralism thus demands that all faiths must strive toward a relational understanding of the distinctiveness of their truth claims based on their scriptures. It means that we define and express our faith and self-understanding "not over against other people" and their religious commitments "but in relation to them."

Toward a Relational View of Christ

What do I mean by a relational view of Christ or a relational distinctiveness of God's revelation in Jesus Christ? To state it succinctly, it is the Christian conviction that the fullness of what God wants to make known to humans is distinctly focused in Jesus Christ; but to increase the depth of the picture, Christians have to relate what they have in Jesus to the mysterious work of God among other religious faiths, in so far as God is the creator of all. This does not mean that we engage in a comparative study of the person and ministry of Jesus in relation to the saviors, prophets, and divinities of other religions. Similarities among the birth narratives of Jesus, Moses, Gautama Buddha, Krishna, and the Qur'anic Jesus have often been cited by many, as have been similarities in the teachings of great religious figures of history. Such similarities in the biographies of religious founders or their teachings may be instructive for our understanding of religious faiths, but they are coincidental to a Christian understanding of Jesus. We therefore need to rethink our faith in relational terms, searching our Scriptures and our theological heritage for clues that might help us to respond intelligibly to the questions before us. As we explore our scriptures in dialogue with others, our study becomes spiritual and relational as well as intellectual.

One of the central affirmations of our faith is that "the Word became flesh" in Jesus of Nazareth. In the Christian reckoning, the divine assumption of human nature, that is, the incarnation of the divine in the historical person of Jesus Christ, is an act of redemption of *all* humanity. The divine identification with creation in the incarnation of Jesus is *intrinsically* an act of salvation, redemption, and reconciliation of all humanity and the created world. God in Christ not only enters into the lives of *all* people but also shares in the sufferings and struggles of humanity. In Christ, God has indeed embraced *all* humanity and draws all humanity unto Godself. Christ died for all humanity. The cross, therefore, represents a new articulation of God's covenant with all humanity, not unlike the covenant God made with Noah after the flood (Genesis 8:21). Put differently, in the event of the cross, the passion history of Jesus enters into the passion history of all humanity; the crucified Jesus stands in relation to and in solidarity with the sufferings of all crucified people and the crucified creation (Romans 8:19-25). Thus the religious histories of people and of God's creation cannot remain unaffected by or unrelated to the history of Jesus.

In saying so, I do not mean to suggest that all people are automatically saved whether they acknowledge Christ or not. What I do mean is that the saving work of Christ and God's offer of grace to all humanity is real, and Christians can neither deny or ignore that reality. If that is true, Christians are called to explore how that reality manifests in the lives and beliefs of neighbors of other faiths in dialogue. A relational understanding of the meaning of Jesus Christ without disregarding the distinctive claim of the Christian faith invites Christians to explore how the saving work of Christ manifests in the lives of others.

How is that possible? *Isn't salvation granted only for Christians or those who confess and accept the lordship of Jesus Christ?* I shall now attempt to explore this important question with the help of a story.

The Saved and the Unsaved

Years ago I heard a true story told by a Lutheran missionary from the United States who spent a lifetime serving in India and Sri Lanka. Towards the end of his career in Sri Lanka he had succeeded in converting three young Hindu men to the Christian faith. The day before their baptism, he had invited them for a meal at his home to make sure of their preparedness to accept Christ. During the course of their conversations, one of them said to the missionary that he wanted to visit the Hindu temple for one last time. The missionary was somewhat taken aback by the request. The young man explained, "By the grace of God, I am ready to accept Christ as my Lord and Savior. Before I do, I want to go to the temple one last time and say a word of thanks to the deities I used to worship. Without their help and grace in the past, I would not have come to Christ today."

This is a thought-provoking story at many levels. It suggests a kind of relationality among divergent religious faiths that Christians may have difficulty comprehending. Few Christians would deny that other religious traditions have served or continue to serve as spiritual homes for millions of people. In Christian history other religious traditions have been seen as preparatory for the reception of the Christian message (*preparatio evangelica*). And yet, we have difficulty in comprehending the religious significance, devotional meaning, and ethical guidance they provide for their adherents. This is understandably so because, as noted earlier, we understand our faith from the inside and all others from the outside. Because religious claims put forward by faiths are inevitably internal to their respective self-understanding, rooted in languages, idioms, and worldviews, they often appear unfamiliar, strange, or alien to our Christian worldview. Furthermore, when religious truths are expressed in doctrines, creeds, and other institutional expressions, they become fixed, abstract and absolute. Hence people are prone to uphold their particular apprehension of truth as universal and absolute, and all other articulations are invalid or deficient.

How we understand truth and salvation in a multi-religious society, therefore, is a pertinent question. One way people have responded to this question is to think that there is *some* truth or meaning in the religious claims and understandings of others, but they are only partial, inadequate, or preparatory to their own. Christians have considered Judaism as preparatory to the Christian revelation; and, in a similar way, Islam claims to supersede Jewish and Christian revelations. The Lutheran theological tradition acknowledges the reality of God's hidden presence in creation and the validity of God's law operative in the world. Thus other religions possess some elements of indirect or incomplete knowledge of divine truth, but they are deficient as they lack a "revealed" knowledge of God's grace in Jesus Christ. Such theological assessments motivated the modern missionary enterprise to conceive of Christian faith as the fulfillment of the aspirations of other cultures and religions. A "theology of displacement" of other religious beliefs and traditions has long dominated Christian relations with others. The story narrated above could be understood in this manner. A linear understanding of salvation history or a "progressive revelation" of God in human history has been influential in much of Christian thinking, as well as in the thinking of Muslims and others.

> We understand our faith from the inside and all others from the outside. Religious claims of others therefore are often unfamiliar or strange to our Christian worldview.
>
> A "theology of displacement" of other religious beliefs has long dominated Christian relations with other people.

The missionary story could also be read as a profound acknowledgment of the reality of grace in the Hindu religion in the experience of the young man and not a total rejection of his prior faith. It seems he was unwilling to let go of the deities he worshipped although his religious preference had now shifted. It is indeed hard to give up one's previous faith commitments because they are part of one's life and formation. Rejection of one's ancestral faith in many cultures is tantamount to rejection of one's own ancestors! Furthermore, in most religious faiths of Asia, there is no insistence on a singular or exclusive understanding of truth. In other words, truth is not a matter of either/or, right or wrong, a correct view or an incorrect view. Truth is relational and is discerned in particular moments or contexts. Truth is a matter of perspective, how you look at reality and from what vantage point (as in the Buddhist story of blind men feeling an elephant and describing it according to their perceptions). Every viewpoint is a view from a point. One's discernment of truth in a particular context or at a given point in history therefore cannot have exclusive validity. It can indeed be valid but not exclusive, unique, or final. Perhaps such a perspective may have informed the young man's confession in the story. The idea of a singular revelation of God, given once and for all, is thus questioned or rejected by many in light of the Hindu view of multiple incarnations (*avatar*) of God.

The story also makes us ponder about our theology of grace. In my mother tongue there is a saying: "God gives grace freely, but custodians of tradition are prone to withhold it." Though few Christians would disagree that divine grace is a free gift of God, many would have difficulty in acknowledging the reality of grace in the experiences of people of other religious traditions. Our received theologies have contrasted Christianity as a religion of grace, whereas other religious traditions are human attempts at works-righteousness or religions of law rather than grace. Such characterizations of the faith and beliefs of others are misleading or problematic. It is a genuine temptation to label or define others according to our preconceived views by using our theological measuring stick rather than hearing what others actually believe according to their self-understandings of faith. Muslims, for example, always invoke the name of God as "merciful and compassionate." In Hindu traditions (especially in strands of Vaishnavism) and in some branches of Mahayana Buddhism, human dependence on divine mercy is central. Whether religions have an articulated understanding of divine grace or not, the reality and the experience of God's grace is undeniably present among all people. Not to believe so is contrary to a Christian understanding of grace as a free gift of God.

I have touched on the issues of grace, truth, and salvation somewhat cursorily as a helpful introduction to the issue of the saving significance of Christ in relation to other religious traditions. A lot of Christians are truly burdened about the salvation of people who do not profess Jesus Christ as their Savior. In popular Christianity, salvation is often thought of in terms of eternal destiny of the individual's life after death. Some are more obsessed about "furniture in heaven or the temperature in hell." This, of course, is a caricature. More seriously, Christian tradition has long insisted that "outside the church there is no salvation" or "there is no salvation outside of Christ." In doing Bible studies in congregations, I often encounter people expressing similar sentiments. When asked the questions—What do you mean by "salvation"? How would you know that there are no other paths to salvation?—people are often lost or hard pressed to give an intelligent answer other than to cite the familiar biblical texts that we reviewed earlier.

We need to be clear that the term "salvation" is specifically a Christian term and therefore not really commensurable or applicable to what other faiths consider as the ultimate goal of life. Christians therefore would be disappointed if they are looking to other faith adherents for an explicit articulation of salvation that coheres with Christian views. Different religious traditions use different religious terms or categories (enlightenment, liberation, *nirvana*, *moksha*, eternal life in heaven, realization of oneness with the ultimate reality, harmony with nature, and so on) to describe the ultimate end of religious life. They don't mean the same, nor are the religious paths they prescribe to the attainment of the ultimate purpose in life the same. Given such profound differences among religious faiths, it would be misleading to think of religious faiths as "different ways to salvation." It is equally misleading to pose the question, "Are you saved?" to people of other faiths, since the question implies an imposition of a Christian view of salvation upon others. In fact, the question may not even make sense to others, because they do not subscribe to a Christian view of salvation. If religions represent different means and point to different ends for human life, how are we to think of the Christian understanding of "salvation" in relation to people of other faiths?

Salvation as Reconciliation

It is not necessary here to review what "salvation" means in the Hebrew Scriptures or in the New Testament, except to note there is *no singular understanding* of what salvation means in Scriptures. However, the New Testament witness is unified in its affirmation that the life, death, and resurrection of Jesus Christ has saving significance for the whole world. But there is a profound diversity in understanding or grasping the saving significance of the Christ event. There are many meanings of salvation in scriptures employing different metaphors and displaying various cultural understandings. They include justification, redemption, sacrifice, sin offering, ransom, forgiveness, fullness of life, wholeness, victory over death and the devil, resurrection of the dead, hope for eternal life, reconciliation, and redemptive suffering. In different ages and divergent cultural settings one or more metaphors gained prominence and others faded into the background. Each of these metaphors presents serious challenges and problems for our understanding. No single metaphor can thus capture the fullness of salvation offered in Christ. Because of this profound diversity and complexity in the Christian understanding of salvation, the church has never made an official pronouncement about what constitutes salvation.

The church has indeed made doctrinal pronouncements about the "person of Jesus Christ" (the divine and human natures of Christ and their unity) in the Nicene and Athanasian Creeds but did not venture into making a definitive statement about the meaning of the "work of Christ" or the benefits of Christ's work. This may be shocking to many and may contradict what we hear in sermons expounding the meaning of the death and resurrection of Jesus Christ. Theologians of the church have indeed proffered many theories and explanations of the significance of Jesus' death and resurrection "for us and for our salvation" (theories of atonement) and how salvation becomes a present reality in the life of the believer, but they are all human attempts to comprehend a mystery that truly transcends human comprehension! These divergent understandings should not be seen as contradicting one another but as complementary. No one expression or metaphor fully and adequately expresses the meaning of salvation.

> The church has never made an official pronouncement of what constitutes "salvation."

> How one defines the problem of the human condition determines the meaning of "salvation."

> The essence of a Christian view of salvation has to do with right relationship with God and our neighbors.

For most Christians, our understanding of salvation is deeply personal and is grounded in our individual experiences of God, Christ, and the Holy Spirit, irrespective of their denominational affiliation. Christians are therefore prone to think of salvation in personal terms, often more narrowly in terms of salvation of one's soul or an assured entry into heaven. But the essence of a Christian view of salvation has to do with *right relationship with God and our neighbors* (which includes our relationship with the created world). It is the Christian conviction that God in Christ has restored a right relationship with God through the offer of grace and forgiveness so that we too may become bearers of God's grace and forgiveness in all our relationships. Salvation, in Christian understanding, is not purely individual but has profound communal implications.

Some evangelistically-minded Christians frequently ask the question, "Are you saved?" The answer depends on what you mean by "saved" or what we are "saved from." How one defines the problem of the human condition determines the meaning of salvation. The various biblical metaphors about the meaning of salvation offer different analyses of the human predicament. Similarly, other religious faiths too propose different diagnoses of the human situation and offer different solutions to them. Christians tend to assume, for example, that our understanding of "original sin" is a common human predicament shared by all. Surely, others also recognize the reality of human failures, moral shortcomings, mistakes, evil in their midst, but not as a permanent (ontological) condition. Muslims (and, for that matter, Jews) don't subscribe to the Christian notion of original sin as something congenitally inherited from Adam and Eve. If one doesn't believe in the idea of original sin, there is no need for a savior or a divine mediator between God and humans. To cite another example, Buddhists diagnose the human situation in terms of "suffering" (*dukkha*) and therefore liberation (*nirvana*) from bondage to suffering as the ultimate goal of life, similar to the Hindu view of life caught up in the cycle of birth, death, and reincarnation (*karma and samsara*). Buddhists therefore do not consider Buddha as a divine mediator, nor do Hindus consider their gods as saviors in the Christian sense.

> The Christian understanding of human existence, its bondage to sin and its need for a savior is not shared by other religious faiths.
>
> Christians must resist the temptation to play God, to be the arbiters of other people's salvation or their eternal destinies. That is God's business and not ours!

The point that I am trying to make is that it would be presumptuous on our part to assume that all people think like us, share our religious presuppositions or our prescriptions to health and wholeness in life. That people of other religious traditions have different analyses of the human situation and different ways for responding to them need not perturb us. Despite our own faith commitments to salvation in Jesus Christ alone, who are we to judge the validity or the invalidity of the faith claims of others? My own struggles with the question of salvation of people who do not profess Jesus as the Savior have led me to the conclusion that Christians must resist the temptation to play God, to be the arbiters of other people's salvation or their eternal destinies. That is God's business and not ours!

And yet, my experience of God's work in Jesus Christ has constantly led me to search for the saving significance of my Lord and Savior for others who do not share my Christian beliefs and convictions. Among the many metaphors that I alluded to earlier and the least emphasized in Christian history and theology is the metaphor of Christ as the reconciler. I am drawn to this metaphor because in the religiously, culturally, economically, and politically divided world of today, the message and mission of Christians and the church is about reconciliation. As St. Paul eloquently states,

> So if anyone is in Christ, there is a new creation: everything old has passed away; see everything has become new! All this is from God, who reconciled us to himself through Christ, and has given us the ministry of reconciliation; that is, in Christ God was reconciling the world to himself, not counting the trespasses against them, and entrusting the message of reconciliation to us. So we are ambassadors of Christ, since God is making his appeal through us; we entreat you on behalf of Christ, be reconciled to God (2 Corinthians 5:17-20, NRSV).

I take considerable comfort in St. Paul's words that "God was in Christ reconciling the world to himself." Setting aside the gendered language Paul uses in referring to God, salvation is about mending the broken relationships between God and humanity, between humans irrespective of race, ethnicity, culture, and religion, and between God and the whole creation. Our experience of salvation in Jesus Christ is intimately bound up with the larger reconciling work of God in the world. The relational distinctiveness of Jesus as God's revelation therefore is inherently related to the reconciling work of God carried forward in our ministry and mission of reconciliation in the world.

Such a conviction may free us to engage boldly in dialogical relationships with people of other living faiths. However, we should not be too quick to offer definitive theological answers to the question of how the saving work of Christ is related to the faith and beliefs of others. Our answer to that question must be *discovered dialogically* rather than *resolved theologically*. The experience of divine grace in the testimonies and lived practices of others may provide us clues, however ambiguous they may be, for comprehending the mysterious saving presence of Christ in the lives of others. Inter-religious engagement today is simultaneously a call to discern God's mysterious work in the world and a commitment to extend Christ's ministry of reconciliation among all people.

> Our experience of salvation in Jesus Christ is intimately bound up with the larger reconciling work of God in the world.
>
> The Lutheran conviction that God's activity is simultaneously hidden and revealed in creation provides a theological space for engaging with others.

Such a posture is grounded in our theological heritage. It is a foundational assumption of Lutheran theology that God's revelation is *simultaneously* hidden and revealed; God's activity *simultaneously* occurs through the work of God's left hand and right hand; the saving activity of God takes place *simultaneously* through law and gospel; Christ is *simultaneously* divine and human; the Christian is *simultaneously* saint and sinner. This Lutheran dialectic of *simul* (Latin for "simultaneously"), if taken seriously, may provide us an insight into our contemporary dialogical engagements. It provides us the necessary grounding or theological space for acknowledging the reality of God's presence in the faith and beliefs of others while affirming the centrality of God's revelation in Christ. Because God is *simultaneously* hidden in the world and yet decisively revealed in Christ alone, Christians can firmly hold on to Christ *alone* and yet confidently explore the hidden work of God in the world of religions. The implicit tension between God's revelation in Jesus Christ *alone* and God's hidden work in the religions of the world cannot be theologically squared away, but we must live in that tension.[7]

---

7 For a fuller articulation of a Lutheran perspective on the theology of religions, see J. Paul Rajashekar, "Rethinking Lutheran Engagement with Religious Plurality, " in *Transformative Theological Perspectives,* ed. Karen I. Bloomquist (Minneapolis, Lutheran University Press, 2009), 105-116; J. Paul Rajashekar, "Luther as a Resource for Christian Dialogue with Other Religions,". in *The Oxford Handbook of Martin Luther's Theology,* eds. Robert Kolb, Irene Dingle and L'Ubomir Batka (London, Oxford University Press), 435-446. Also, Peter Pettit, "Christ Alone, the Hidden God and Lutheran Exclusivism, *Word and World,* XI, Number 2, Spring 1991: 190-198.

Christian Mission in a Pluralistic Society

There still remains one important question that needs to be addressed: Do Christians have a mission among people of other faiths? If God and Christ are already present or in some mysterious way related to people of other faiths, what is the point of Christian witnessing and evangelizing in the world? Should we set aside the biblical mandate (Matthew 28:18-20) to make disciples of all nations? Don't we have a message to share and invite people into Christian fellowship?

Christians do have a profound message to share. This has been the foundation of Christian mission and evangelism in the course of Christian history. The Christian faith has been planted in all continents as a result of the faithful witness of innumerable disciples, evangelists, missionaries, and believers in Christ. I too was an evangelist among Muslims in South India even before I was engaged in Christian broadcasting. But over the years I have become more cautious and circumspect about aggressive forms of mission and evangelism that many Christians employ. I have noted earlier the religious sensitivities of others toward Christian mission. Here I want to underscore that any form of aggressive or crusading evangelism, denying or denigrating the faith and beliefs of others, is not only inappropriate but also counterproductive in a multi-faith society. I have often found it appalling that Christian evangelists have a tendency to preach a message that is offensive and insensitive to the religious claims of others by vilifying their beliefs. (Think about how Christians feel when the Bible is desecrated by others.) Pastors, too, are often guilty of using other faiths as a foil to uphold the uniqueness of Christian faith in their sermons. Christian witness is a *positive witness* to what God has done in Jesus Christ and *not a negative witness* of maligning or vandalizing the religious beliefs and claims of others. We don't need to deny or denigrate other names or saviors in order to uphold our Savior!

Christians need to ask seriously the question: Why do we engage in Christian proclamation? Is it because of our obedience to a biblical mandate? Is it a law that we must obey, or a joyful response to the experience of God's grace? Why is this particular mandate ("Go therefore and make disciples of all nations.") taken so seriously while we choose to ignore a whole lot of other biblical demands (such as the teachings of Jesus in the Sermon on the Mount)? In some Christian circles, "Reaching the unreached" is another slogan frequently employed to mobilize cross-cultural evangelism. The slogan prompts the question, "Unreached by whom?" Just because a Christian evangelist or missionary (from the West) has not

> Why do we engage in Christian proclamation? Is it because of our obedience to a biblical mandate or a joyful response to gospel?
>
> Christian witness is a positive witness to what God has done in Jesus Christ and not a negative witness of vilifying the religious beliefs of others.

preached to people in some distant corner of the world does not mean God has not reached out to them. We are led to ask a further question: What are our assumptions about the faith and beliefs of others when we engage in the proclamation of the gospel? Do we engage because we assume God is absent in the lives of others or because God is present among them? These are some critical questions that require further thought in a pluralistic society.

In the preceding reflections I have noted the boundless love and grace of God operative in the lives of all people, and noted that Christian understanding of the love and mercy manifest in Jesus Christ is not exclusive but relational. A relational understanding of our faith does not necessarily exclude Christian witness to faith but rather invites it. This may come as a surprise to the reader of this reflection. The reasons are many.

First, in a multi-faith society, where different faiths make exclusive claims for their understanding of truth and for the distinctiveness of their perception of God's revelation or their religious worldview, an implicit, if not explicit, question is raised: "By what authority do you (Christians and others) make such and such a claim?" As noted earlier, citing scriptural texts of our own tradition alone can neither persuade nor make sense to others. Others too can cite their authoritative texts or scriptures. Beyond citing texts of authority, Christians and others are challenged to explain what their faith commitments mean for them personally in daily life and communally. Pluralism demands that in the presence of the other we are publicly accountable for our faith. Making definitive or absolute statements without offering a reasoned articulation of our faith is futile. The First Letter of Peter states the point rather eloquently: "Always be ready to make your defense to anyone who demands from you an accounting for the hope that is in you; yet do it with gentleness and reverence" (1 Peter 3:15-16, NRSV).

Second, witnessing to our faith is not a one-way street. Christians are fond of singing the hymn, "I love to tell the story," in our churches, and no doubt we do have a story to tell. No one can question the right and freedom of Christians to tell their story. But by the same token, do neighbors of other faiths also have their stories to tell? Are we prepared to listen to their stories? Witnessing in a pluralistic society is a two-way street. Christian dialogue with people of other faiths is not a disguised monologue! Without listening to and understanding the religious experiences and claims of others and their stories, Christians engaging in mission and evangelism run the risk of becoming religious propagandists or marketing strategists focused on gaining adherents to our faith. Christian witnessing is about practicing the reconciling work of God in the world. It means that we are called to risk crossing religious, social, and political boundaries that divide people to experience the full humanity of those on the other side. It also implies that Christians challenge the polarizing ideologies that fuel distrust, fear, and violence in our world. Practicing the reconciling work of Christ suggests "being with" those who suffer and are in pain, especially those who are persecuted for their faith and beliefs, in order to create the possibility of re-entry into a reconciling human community. Mission today is a multifaceted vocation of risking Christ for the sake of Christ! In listening to the stories and testimonies of others in dialogue, we discern the mysterious work of God in the midst of all faiths. We may even discover the hidden presence of Christ (cf. Matthew 25) in the lives and beliefs of people of other faiths!

> Pluralism demands that in the presence of the other we are publicly accountable for our faith and therefore invites Christian witness in dialogue with others.

> Christian witness today is about practicing the reconciling work of God in the world.

> Witnessing in a pluralistic society is a two-way street. Christian dialogue with people of other faiths is not a disguised monologue!

Third, our context not only invites mutual witnessing, but also urges us to go beyond the prevailing notions of a "theology of neutrality," that is, the view that all faiths are the same or equally valid. Religious plurality in our midst is not a static reality, as if people are destined to live in their own religious/secular ghettos. Ours would be a comatose world if people had no freedom to shift their beliefs and religious affiliation. Many in Western societies have opted to belong to many religious faiths rather than a singular allegiance to one faith. Given this reality, the possibility of religious conversion in society can neither be ruled out nor deemed inappropriate. People should have the freedom to convert or cross over from one faith to another in a religiously plural world without coercion. Needless to say, from a Christian standpoint, conversion to the Christian faith is entirely the work of the Holy Spirit. We should rejoice when people are drawn to the Christian faith (and shout out loud, *Subhanuallah*, "Glory be to God") but we need not begrudge or feel burdened when others claim that their chosen faith is sufficient and meaningful to attain the ultimate goal in life.

Learning to Be Guests in the Midst of Others

It should be obvious by now that my reflections are grounded on the view that religious pluralism in our midst has to be actively valued rather than passively tolerated. Admittedly, I have not addressed all the questions that readers of this essay may pose. I have only sought to build some theological bridges between people of divergent faiths and to create a *theological space* for engaging in conversations, while affirming the Christian conviction about the revelation of God in Jesus Christ and at same time honoring and respecting the faith of others. Christians need not be ashamed of their faith commitments, nor should we consider the religious claims of others as a threat to the truth and integrity of our faith. Many in Western societies today are drawn to the spiritual practices of other faiths because of curiosity or spiritual hunger. Increasing numbers of people (the so called "nones") have expressed no singular allegiance to any one faith, and some have opted for multiple religious belongings. The phenomenon of religious "syncretism" (mixing of diverse beliefs) may be far more widely practiced than publically acknowledged. Religious pluralism in our midst invariably challenges, implicitly or explicitly, all claims to "religious self-sufficiency" and therefore mutual appreciation and enrichment is a necessary aspect of contemporary life. Rather than feeling intimidated by religious plurality, our engagement with other faiths provides a splendid opportunity for us to learn about ourselves both individually and communally. In relating with others, we rediscover our religious identity and deepen our faith.

> Religious pluralism in our midst has to be actively valued rather than passively tolerated.
>
> In a pluralistic world people are strangers to one another and therefore we are all guests and hosts to one another.
>
> Practicing a "theology of hospitality" means learning to be guests in the midst of others.

These reflections began with my struggles to understand and interpret the prayers of others. It is still my fervent hope that people of all faiths pray in unison, "Pray— that we may pray together." This is not to advocate some form of "syncretism" or the creation of a single "world religion." Far from it! Rather, it is a call to recognize our shared humanity and the need to create a *shared theological space* that may promote mutual reverence and peaceful coexistence. Sharing a theological space with others raises myriad of profound questions as this essay has shown: questions about our understanding of God, God's relationship with others, the distinctive relatedness of Jesus Christ, the meaning of Christ's work of salvation, issues of scripture, the importance of dialogue as a ministry of reconciliation, and rethinking the nature of Christian mission today. In these reflections I have attempted to share my personal experiences and struggles in responding to such difficult questions—not to offer definitive theological pronouncements, but as helpful directions for Christian engagement with people of other faiths. Needless to say, some theological questions will always remain unanswered on this side of eternity. However, as I have indicated at the outset, *answers to some questions cannot be resolved theologically but only discovered dialogically*, that is, in our engagement with people who profess other faiths. I want to conclude this chapter with one additional remark.

In a globalized and yet religiously divided world with contesting faith claims, we may well consider ourselves as fellow pilgrims and sojourners in search of God's mercy in our human predicament. We are humans and in need of God's love and mercy, and that propels us to the practice of a "theology of hospitality" to one another.

What I mean by the word "hospitality" is not just about Christians being the hosts and others as our guests (as commonly understood in congregations welcoming guests). Hospitality is a biblical word meaning "love of the stranger." In a pluralistic world people are indeed strangers to one another, and therefore all are guests and hosts to one another. As fellow pilgrims and seemingly strangers to one another, we have a long way to go in *learning to be guests in the midst of others*, irrespective of our beliefs and faith commitments (cf. Hebrews 13:1-2). Being a guest is more vulnerable than being a host. It means to "take our shoes off" as we enter the homes and sacred places of others as their guests. Learning from others means putting ourselves in another's place, wearing their shoes and seeing ourselves as others. It means to listen to what others believe and profess. Listening is a profound mark of respect for the other. We can be transformed by listening, by seeing others as they see us, and by genuinely "being" for others and "with" others in all our relationships. In recognizing the otherness of the other we may discover who we are, what we are, and our true religious identity. Claims of religious exclusivism or particularity may be necessary or inevitable for our self-identity. But our desire to demonstrate the love of God in relation to people who differ from us requires courage, certainty, and a commitment to a deeper understanding of our own faith and identity in a pluralistic world.

To Have Lost Our Saltiness

Joseph Kempf, Augsburg College, Class of 2016

"(And Jesus said) You are the salt of the earth; but if salt has lost its taste, how can its saltiness be restored? It is no longer good for anything, but is thrown out and trampled under foot" (Matthew 5:13).

You are . . . a people of faith. You are . . . a city on a hill. You are . . . the salt of the earth. In the Sermon on the Mount, Jesus calls his followers salt, of all things! Don't get me wrong, salt is delicious and needed. But we could be something great! We could be legends, we could be a mountain. Instead, Jesus charges us with salt. While there are numerous interpretations of what exactly is meant by being the salt of the earth, I personally hold this verse in the Gospel of Matthew to indicate how followers of Jesus should engage in the world. I am going to do this with a little bit of chemistry.

I wanted to be scholarly and a little rebellious, so I researched what "salt of the earth" means. According to the Wikipedia page devoted to Matthew 5:13, "Salt itself, sodium chloride, is extremely stable and cannot lose its flavor. . . . [then some author notes] Jesus is 'not giving a chemistry lesson'." I'm almost a little offended. Who are they to decide when chemistry stops? If there is one thing I have learned at Augsburg College, chemistry never stops. Since Jesus clearly was not teaching chemistry, I think I will step up to the plate, so to speak.

I'm sure all of you are familiar enough with cooking. You know with all of your might that oil and water will never mix, no matter how much you stir. Oil is simply too big for water to take on. Long chains of carbons and hydrogens are not attractive to water's oxygen and hydrogen combo. Maybe for too long, Christians have become oily in practice and deed. We have become too engrossed with our beliefs, what road or beliefs lead to heaven, or what a specific passage actually means. If water represents the world, frequently we just sit on top, looking at the world below us but never submerge ourselves. We may see our neighbors, many of various religions, but we seldom act. What we need is a radical shift in ideas and our approach to other religions. But Jesus doesn't call us the "oil of the earth"; we are the "salt of the earth"! You know perfectly well what salt does in water: It breaks apart and fully involves itself in water's affairs.

An important thing to note is that the salt is never destroyed in this transaction, and neither is the water. Often what holds us back from working or engaging in interfaith dialogue and service is the simple fact that we are afraid of losing our faith—of changing for the worse or even of where to begin. Likewise, we must remember that the very people we are called to serve are also stubborn in faith and belief. Interfaith work is so powerful because of the basic tenet that we are not trying to convert the other. It is a waste of energy. Here, too, we often fail. But of course these actions can be learned. We are called to engage the world and serve our neighbor. How much longer are we going to separate ourselves from this sacred service?

Interfaith service and dialogue are important and needed work—important because we are called to live in this world, not as only Christians or only Muslims, but as humankind; to serve rather than to be served; to engage instead of fall asleep to the cries of the world.

I have come to the opinion that the Gospels don't need much prodding in order to reveal to Christians that interfaith service is a necessary project. Many people continue to approach interfaith service and dialogue like a nice option, a creative and unique box to explore for its own sake. While interfaith work is altogether important and requires a well of creativity, the Gospels call—no—*wail* out to us to serve and engage our neighbor. We must wander the world around us, desperately and endlessly listening to the calls of the poor and oppressed—not regardless of their religion, but *because* of their religion. There is no doubt that rich and powerful work can be done when we grasp the hands of our friends and neighbors and use faith or beliefs as a starting point and cornerstone to our work. I engage in interfaith service because the Scriptures in my tradition call me to be first in service and generosity, and truly take on the title of salt of the earth.

This sermon was delivered to the Augsburg Corporation, a group of congregation members who have ties with Augsburg College. The original topic given was, "Why interfaith work matters." Back in January 2015, I studied abroad in El Salvador, a deeply religious country afflicted by genocide, civil war, and violence. Personally, the gospel as preached by Monsignor Romero in El Salvador seemed so rich and saturated with God. In his messages were hope, concern for the poor, and deep forgiveness; they have since haunted me. These travels and experiences directly informed this sermon.

Conflict During Dinner: Intra-Religious Dispute Solved Through Interfaith Discussion

Caleb Arndt, California Lutheran University, Class of 2016

A couple years ago, a couple of dear friends of mine and I decided to go to out to get a bite after an interfaith event in which we participated on campus. Because one of my friends (we'll call her "Ella") is Muslim, we decided it would be a good idea to check out the local halal options. My other friend, "Miles," suggested a pizza place that had just opened up in the next city over. I had never been to a halal restaurant before, so I wasn't exactly sure what to expect.

After a pleasant drive full of engaging conversation, we arrived at the pizza parlor and proceeded to walk up to the counter. The owner was wearing a traditional *thawb*, a common dress for male Muslims, and appeared to be quite surprised that there were two non-Muslims in his restaurant. Miles and I ordered first and sat ourselves down at the table adjacent to the register. Ella finished ordering and joined us; she seemed rather deflated. I inquired why she seemed so down, and she explained what had just happened to her.

You see, a few years prior to this event, Ella decided to start wearing *hijab*, a covering many Muslim women wear in accordance with tradition. This decision is often very momentous and sentimental to the individual, and is a demonstration of commitment to the faith of Islam. Apparently, Ella had paid for her food with her card and was required to show her identification with it. In her driver's license, she was not wearing hijab. The owner looked down at the picture and then back at Ella. "You should really retake this photo while wearing hijab. That's the good Muslim thing to do."

Ella is a progressive, feminist, interfaith advocate, and a devout Muslim. Normally she would be the kind to stand up for herself, but she was utterly devastated in this situation. It is one thing to have someone from another faith background criticize you based on ignorance, but it is a much tougher pill to swallow when someone of your own faith does it.

After hearing this story, Miles and I decide to confront the owner of the establishment. We did not berate him, condemn him, yell at him, nor demand he apologize. We spent about twenty minutes in dialogue with him explaining how there are different motivations and perspectives when it comes to wearing hijab, and how not updating a license picture doesn't make you a bad Muslim. We stressed that being "a good Muslim" is a matter of perspective, not an objective claim. While the owner may not have agreed with everything we were saying, he remained in conversation with us and respected our opinions. Miles and I said goodbye and met Ella outside. Shortly after, we bought Ella frozen yogurt.

This conversation didn't completely reform this man's beliefs or get him to apologize. However, that's not what interfaith is about. In fact, that is contrary to what interfaith is all about. It's not about proving one way is right or wrong, it's about understanding as many perspectives as you can and finding commonalities that can help to grow inter-religious relationships with the end goal of helping humanity as a whole.

Interfaith and the Impact It Has Had on My Lutheran Faith

I was involved in the interfaith movement at California Lutheran University (CLU). The student president at the time brought me on board after I had expressed interest in interfaith work during a student senate retreat early in my freshman year. I immediately fell in love with the cross-cultural communication, the emphasis on story-telling, and the potential it had for service opportunities.

Fast forward to my second semester, and I was now officially a member of the newly-created Interfaith Allies at CLU. My excitement and eagerness were palpable; I knew we were going to accomplish amazing feats. However, our first official event happened to be our biggest. Every year, the Interfaith Youth Core (IFYC) has a national, collegiate challenge called "Better Together Day." This is a day dedicated to spreading interfaith engagement and cooperation. The status quo for this day is to put together some sort of event to draw attention to interfaith as well as adding a service component. Since it was our first ever year attempting this, we decided to follow suit.

We created a campaign called "Water Wise with Interfaith Allies." It was focused on water conservation and encouraged students, faculty, and staff to donate the money that they would have spent on water that week to an organization that builds wells in various African countries. The plan was great; however, putting it into action proved much more difficult. The Interfaith Allies started running into many roadblocks, and we were concerned if we would finish in time.

At the time, I was heavily involved with Lord of Life, the Lutheran student congregation on campus. After talking with my fellow allies, we decided that the best course of action would be to ask for their help, as well as involve the Community Service Center. The response was overwhelming. We were able to finish the event prep and market to a large audience. In fact, CLU won the best overall campus engagement award from IFYC that year.

This response that the Lutheran community at CLU had and continues to have confirmed to me why I am so proud of my Lutheran tradition. Now years later, I see more and more Lutherans catching on to the necessity of interfaith involvement in our globalized society; I really applaud what the ELCA has done. Being living examples of love and community beyond societal expectations is exactly what being a Lutheran, or any human being for that matter, should strive to do.

A statistic I hear associated constantly with millennials is one that cites the sharp drop in religious activism amongst this age group. Churches, mosques, temples, etc., are all reporting decreasing numbers in my age group. However, I do not necessarily think that this

Jamie, Shireen, and Rebecca share a moment during the Interfaith Youth Core #BeBlue #Better Together day in April 2013, gaining pledges for interfaith support while raising awareness for the upcoming Water Wise/Green Week campaign.

is a negative thing. I believe a good deal of this comes from my generation's stubbornness against doing something just for the sake of doing it. For example, too often did I hear kids growing up complain about how their parents made them go to church, even when they didn't want to go. Unfortunately, I think this mentality caused a negative association with organized religion for a lot of people in my generation—a generation that already has a strong sense of individualism and self-discovery.

However, the reason I believe this could be a good thing is that it has led many millennials to look into other religions and cultures before deciding which faith tradition they want to be a part of, if at all. This kind of education and exposure has created an intelligent, socially accepting, and religiously diverse group of young people, many of whom are incredibly informed and active about social justice.

I believe this is why the interfaith movement has really taken off with this age group. We are now more aware of people from different faith backgrounds than ever before. Not only this, but we have more day-to-day interactions among people of different races, religions or non-religions, and socioeconomic groups. The stigmas are slowly going away, and there is a growing, concerted social justice effort led by my generation.

Interfaith in an Environment of Lutheran Tradition

Rebecca Cardone, California Lutheran University, Class of 2013

I may not be Lutheran myself, but because California Lutheran University (CLU) is rooted in Lutheran tradition, it encourages open dialogue about faith and philosophy, which makes us stronger in our purpose and vocation. That language flows very easily now, but in 2011 students did not know how to encourage religious diversity while preserving the middle name of the university we loved. I was a sophomore and a member of the Secular Student Alliance (SSA) at CLU. The club discussed "what you believe and why," followed by site visits to learn about world religions and the other's convictions. We challenged each other to be vulnerable, question everything, and respect each other's differences.

In that spirit, we noticed that one line of the preamble in the student government constitution included the phrase, "to further Christian growth." Understandably, a Christian university wants its student organizations to further Christian growth through direct or indirect activities. Despite this phase, CLU had an active Hillel and other student-initiated and faculty-sponsored organizations that celebrated religious diversity. Some students felt that they were unintentionally excluded from the student body because of their religious or philosophical beliefs.

Members of the SSA, who were religiously diverse and not only secular, proposed an amendment to this constitution with phrasing less structurally marginaliz-

Interfaith Allies used blue wristbands, initiated as part of the InterFaith Youth Core's "#BeBlue #BetterTogether" campaign, to show solidarity with those who pledged to develop interfaith efforts in their daily lives and at California Lutheran University. They received more pledges in one day than any other campus in the USA, and they won Best Overall Campaign for the 2013 Better Together Awards.

ing of non-Christian students at CLU. But we were ill-prepared for the media and community backlash. Not only did the student-wide vote fail, but we also unintentionally jeopardized relations with alumni, the ELCA, and the university administration. CLU became polarized between those fearful of the "slippery slope of secularism" and those seeking greater inclusivity.

Why does it matter? Globally, religion is often manipulated to be a façade for seemingly intractable conflicts. If we can build interfaith relationships in the microcosm of CLU, we could change the world— or at least change hearts and minds in our home communities. We needed a holistic campaign that empowered stakeholders at all levels to take ownership of interfaith involvements at CLU.

Thanks to a generous grant from the philanthropic Vesper Society, a core team of faculty and students attended two of the Interfaith Youth Core's Interfaith Leadership Institutes in 2012, and we launched the "Interfaith Allies" that fall. The Interfaith Allies at CLU were unique from the other campus organizations and the student clubs. We decidedly were not a club at all, to avoid drawing a distinction between members and others, or between students and stakeholders. The Interfaith Allies pointedly partnered with existing organizations and infiltrated them with intentionally interfaith angles from the "bottom up."

Simultaneously, we joined the university administration for the White House President's Interfaith and Community Service Campus Challenge from the "top down," to ensure that CLU's religious diversity was engaged and appreciated through tending our common ground. With comprehensive interfaith efforts, the Interfaith Allies initiated a Water Wise campaign during Green Week in April 2013 to bring interfaith to the fore with our community service and sustainability campaign.

With a "fierce urgency of now," the Interfaith Allies' core activities embedded interfaith dialogue, community service, and structural change in partnership with stakeholders throughout the greater CLU community. We broke bread together, shared compassion, and tackled life's big questions with empathy from our own unique identities and perspectives. We built a Water Wise/Green Week campaign that encompassed daily themes on sustainable living, with initiatives ranging from launching zero-waste academic and administrative buildings to embarking on a campaign to become a Fair Trade university. Interfaith Allies were embedded in each of the initiatives as leaders, collaborators, and encouragers. These activities and more focused on *why interfaith matters* at CLU beyond the numbers of diversity at individual and institutional levels.

The structural changes paired with cultural reinforcement allowed for the visible sustainability of the interfaith movement, although they were not without their challenges. With the critical leadership of the campus pastors throughout the campaign, the weekly Chapel Hour became Sabbath Hour, and the Wennes Meditation Chapel became the Wennes Interfaith Meditation Chapel in name and substance. While embracing the foundation of interfaith at the undergraduate level, CLU extended its Lutheran roots and commitment to the ELCA at the postgraduate level as the Board of Regents initiated a merger with the Pacific Lutheran Theological Seminary. Lastly, the preamble to the ASCLU-Government constitution was successfully amended from "to further Christian growth" to "to inspire the maturity of faith and reason in an environment of Lutheran tradition." Rather than polarizing the CLU community with fear and accusations, we had a multilateral interfaith movement underway with a well-articulated discussion of Lutheran identity in higher education, the diversity of the student experience, and a deep appreciation for the founders of the university.

Thanks to the support of passionate faculty allies, we worked through the struggles of student leadership and delegation for efficient, concerted action. Together, we confronted issues that had festered since 2011 within the greater CLU community, proving why a campus climate change for more interfaith harmony was necessary. We transcended the polarization with an interfaith movement in full force. We came to understand, appreciate, and embrace our Lutheran roots as a university that nurtures the interfaith movement "to educate leaders for a globalized society."

Living with the Questions

Darrell Jodock

Religious diversity is not new. The first synagogue in what is now the United States was organized over a hundred years before the American Revolution. Buddhists have lived in California for generations. And, as Jonathan Brockopp observes, the first Muslims probably arrived with Columbus in 1492. The number of non-Christians in the U.S. remains relatively small, and the vast majority of new immigrants are Christians, but the awareness of the presence of people who practice other religions has grown. Christians often know them as neighbors and coworkers. And other religions are frequently in the news.

Though news reports can prompt Christians to want to find out more information about other religions, they unfortunately often have a quite different effect. They create stereotypes that are either false or only marginally accurate. Christians need to remind themselves to be skeptical of those stereotypes. For example, when one hears about the limitations placed on women in Saudi Arabia, it is important to remember that the Wahhabi form of Islam practiced there is not representative of Islam in general. Or when one hears about Sunni–Shi'ite conflict, it is important to remember that Protestants and Catholics were at war in Europe for 300 years after the Reformation—sporadically, yes, but also very destructively. (During the Thirty Years War, Germany lost about one-third of its population). And in the sixteenth and seventeenth centuries Protestant and Catholic Christians tortured their Anabaptist neighbors in particularly gruesome ways. It is also important to remember that the largest numbers of Muslims are not found in the Middle East but in Indonesia, Pakistan, Bangladesh, and India. Those fomenting conflict in the Middle East are a minority within a minority. It is somehow easier for Christians to recognize that the ELCA church member who shot nine persons in the AME Church in Charleston in 2015 is a minority within a minority than it is to recognize that the same is true for the latest Al

Qaeda attack. As Mark Swanson reminds us, the eighth commandment calls us to speak the truth in generous and charitable ways. Stereotypes are not the truth.

Given the increasing awareness of other religions and the inaccuracy of much that we hear, the three main questions of this book take on a new urgency: How should Lutheran Christians engage their non-Christian neighbors? What is a Christian view of other religions? What does it mean to be a Lutheran Christian in a multi-religious world?

How Should Lutheran Christians Engage Their Non-Christian Neighbors?

Regarding the first question, one answer has surfaced repeatedly in the previous chapters. Christians have a calling to practice (or pursue) hospitality. This calling comes from at least two sources. The first is the basic biblical principle that every human being is created in the image of God. This means that every human being is to be treated with respect. One can do so without knowing everything about their religion. Showing hospitality means not relating to them primarily as a representative of a larger group (a Muslim, a Buddhist, etc.) but instead treating each person first as a human being. Given the diversity of persons found within any group or any religion, listening to an individual's story and that individual's outlook is an important way to show respect. The second source of the calling to hospitality is the unmerited grace affirmed in Christianity and especially emphasized within Lutheran circles. In Christ, God takes the initiative to heal our broken relationship. Without any prerequisites, God chooses to treat us with generosity and adopt us. Persons who have been freely graced are called to grace others. Having experienced the generosity of God, we are called to treat others with generosity. The result is radical hospitality. The chapters of this book are full of examples of how this can be done.

> Christians have a calling to practice (or pursue) hospitality . . . and to accept the hospitality of others.

The chapters in this book also emphasize that this hospitality is to be mutual. American Christians tend to want to provide assistance and to fix things. This desire can lead to what some have called an "inclined plane" relationship, when the provider is "up here" and the recipient is "down there." The provider is then in control. By contrast, mutual hospitality puts people on the same plane, side by side or face to face. Standing or walking alongside another is an inherent part of Christianity, for, in Christ, God came to "be with" humans, to experience fully what it means to be human. In the Gospels we see a pattern of Jesus repeatedly "being with" others, as he eats with and visits with a wide variety of individuals, many of whom are not "insiders." He shows compassion and provides assistance, yes, but he also accepts invitations into their homes and receives their hospitality. So, too, it is healthy for Christians not only to practice hospitality but also to accept the hospitality of others. It is a deeply significant way of showing them respect.

Alongside the calling to practice hospitality, another theme can be found in these chapters—namely, the authors acknowledge the discomfort Christians may feel as they begin to interact with persons in another religion. The sources of this discomfort are multiple. One is an anxiety not to offend, and the less one knows about another religion the more acute this can be. The antidote is education and respectful inquiry (of the sort that wants to learn rather than to challenge). Another source is the human tendency to feel most comfortable in a familiar setting and a discomfort with anything unfamiliar. It is important to recognize that the person from another religion is likely also encountering the unfamiliar and is experiencing a similar discomfort. The only way to overcome this typically human feeling is to "hang in there" and gain enough experience so that the unfamiliar gradually becomes familiar. And still another source is theological uncertainty. To this we will return. As we deal with the unfamiliar, perhaps it is helpful to remember the discomfort experienced by numerous biblical figures as they received their calling. It is no accident that "fear not" or "do not be afraid" occurs so frequently in the Bible. God has a way of simultaneously calling us to cross over boundaries into the unfamiliar and reassuring us of God's presence as we undertake this crossing.

> God has a way of simultaneously calling us to cross over boundaries into the unfamiliar and reassuring us of God's presence as we undertake this crossing.

What Is a Christian View of Other Religions?

When we turn to the second question (What is a Christian view of other religions?), the chapters in this book make several important suggestions.

They cite several biblical passages that invite us to re-think our understanding of people in other religions. As two of the chapters remind us, the Good Samaritan is a member of another religion and yet is the most familiar and powerful model of what it means to be a good neighbor. Or we can think of Cyrus, the emperor of Persia (modern-day Iran) and a member of another religion, who is anointed by God to let the

Israelites return from exile (Isaiah 45:1). Or we can think of Jethro, the priest of Midian, who gives Moses valuable advice on how to lead the Israelites (Exodus 18). Or of Abigail, who convinces David not to kill her husband Nabal, who is a Calebite (1 Samuel 25). Or of Rahab, the Canaanite who hides the two spies Joshua sent to find out about Jericho prior to its conquest (Joshua 2). Or of King Abimelech. The list could go on. Again and again, God's blessing comes through someone who is not part of the covenant. The same can happen today.

Another suggestion is to seek out new information that helps us re-think our understanding of familiar biblical passages. In Romans 11, Paul emphatically denies that God has abandoned God's promises to the Jews or rejected his people (see verses 1 and 29). This prompts us to ask to whom the Gospel of John is referring when it says that the parents of the man born blind (John 9:22) and the disciples (John 20:19)—themselves all Jews—were afraid of "the Jews." It turns out that John has in mind the Temple authorities, not Jews in general. As Paul Rajashekar reminds us, John 14:6 (NRSV)—"I am the way, and the truth, and the life"—is an invitation to follow the way of the cross, not to support a crusade that runs roughshod over others. When understood this way, the message is consistent with Philippians 2:5 (NRSV), "Let the same mind be in you that was in Christ Jesus, who, though he was in the form of God, did not regard equality with God as something to be exploited, but emptied himself, taking the form of a slave." The point is this: When we bring to the Bible a new set of questions—questions that were not on the table at the time of the Reformation or at the time European immigrants came to the U.S.—we need to gather the relevant information and be ready to re-think our interpretation of some passages, even those with which we are most familiar. We need to expect to see in them things we had not noticed before.

Another suggestion, more implicit than explicit in the previous chapters, is not to expect to have answers to every question, not to expect to have everything figured out. Each of us needs to be ready to say, "I don't know." After pondering questions about the fate of the Jews who did not accept Jesus as the Christ and not coming up with an answer, Paul throws up his hands in a doxology: "O the depth of the riches and wisdom and knowledge of God! How unsearchable are his judgments and how inscrutable are his ways!" (Romans 11:33, NRSV). The lack of an answer does not undermine Paul's faith. Nor did it undermine Martin Luther's faith. His graduate degree was in biblical studies. He was a life-long student of the Bible. And, for a time, he expected that the Bible would answer every question. When it did not seem to do so, he was troubled.

He then noticed that the psalmists also voiced questions for which they had no answer, as did Jesus (who cried out, "My God, my God, why have you forsaken me?" and did not know when the end of the world would arrive). Luther came to see that people of faith are called to live with unanswered questions. For him, revelation has provided what we need—an understanding of God's attitude toward us, an understanding of God's purpose, and some insight into the character of God—but revelation has not answered every question. Living with unanswered questions is not the same as ignoring them. It means pondering them, seeking additional insights, but not expecting quick or easy or simple answers. Christianity is a way of life. It is relational; it is all about our relationship with God, with other humans, and with the rest of creation. New questions do not undermine our faith; faith is built on trust and does not have everything figured out. We are called to build and to foster whole and healthy relationships, even if our questions are not all answered.

> Christianity is a way of life. It is relational; it is all about our relationship with God, with other humans, and with the rest of creation. New questions do not undermine our faith; faith is built on trust and does not have everything figured out.

Other religions are also a way of life. Beliefs (agreed-upon ideas associated with faith) do not play as prominent a role in most of them as they do in Christianity. So it is best to start a conversation with experiences, practices, and priorities. In what ways does their religious identity open up a sense of wonder, a sense of gratitude, and a sense of connectedness (which are basic aspects of any religion)?

This leads to another suggestion made in this book: not to see oneself engaged in a dialogue between religions, but to see oneself relating to a person whose religious way of life is different from one's own. Just as there are all sorts of Christians who construe the faith in all sorts of ways, so there are all sorts of persons in any other religion who construe that religion in all sorts of ways. Just as not every Christian agrees totally with the statements of Pat Robertson or Pope Francis I, the same is true in other religions, where only the provocateurs are likely to make the news. The focus needs to be on the person or persons we are meeting. Neither they nor we are likely to be well-informed spokespersons for the religion as a whole. Thus, the next step for a Christian participant is a kind of "back and forth" between learning to know the person(s) and learning more about the basics of their religion, so that one can both understand the person(s) and get some sense of how representative their outlook and practices are.

The most basic response to the discomfort Christians experience is the reassurance of those who have already traveled this path. They know that establishing respectful relationships and learning more about another religion are not threats to or betrayals of one's faith. Those who have traveled this path have watched their appreciation for Christianity grow. They begin to notice aspects of it that they had taken for granted or overlooked before. What they already know, they come to understand more deeply. And they discover how much more they have to learn about the Bible and their own faith. Learning more about the other and learning more about one's own faith go hand in hand.

As the chapters make clear, participating in inter-religious dialogue and cooperation does not put an end to witnessing to the good news. Christians who value the good news will let it show. What it does affect is how and when witnessing occurs. The good news is shared as a gift rather than a demand. This is the "how." Inter-religious dialogue involves one limit regarding "when": A dialogical conversation is a time for exploration and not the setting in which to press for conversion. Respecting this limit is important for all involved.

What Does It Mean to Be a Lutheran Christian in a Multi-religious World?

Early in this concluding chapter, three questions were mentioned. The third was this: What does it mean to be a Lutheran Christian in a multi-religious world?

Lutherans are particularly well-equipped for this new experience. For one thing, they celebrate God's unmerited grace. It is a totally undeserved gift. Not only does it heal the relationship broken by sin, but it also promises God's steadfast love in the future. This gives Lutherans the freedom to make mistakes and to err on the side of generosity rather than fearing unforeseen consequences. To repeat what has already been said: The person who has experienced generosity is equipped and expected to show generosity toward others. Lutherans have a solid theological foundation for the practice of radical hospitality.

Before leaving this point, we should notice one common Lutheran theme that sometimes interferes with understanding others. Luther's emphasis on "grace alone" was crafted in response to works righteousness—to a theology that expected humans to do certain things in order to receive grace. His breakthrough came when he saw that God takes the first step to initiate reconciliation. The importance of this discovery prompted Luther himself to interpret other religions in terms of his own struggle. And Lutherans since then have sometimes done the same. So it is important for contemporary Lutherans not to expect that an emphasis on religious or moral practices in another religion is automatically a form of works righteousness. The dynamic may be quite different. Judaism, for example, sees itself as a community chosen by God. Whatever emphasis it gives to good behavior is not to create a relationship with God but to live "response-ably" within the covenant already created by God.

Another way Lutherans are well-equipped for inter-religious relations is that they understand faith to be a matter of trust—trust in God, trust in God's promises—rather than knowledge. Doctrines and beliefs are important, but they are secondary to the quality of relationships, as envisioned in God's overall goal of shalom (whole, healthy relationships between God and humans, among humans, and between humans and nature). Because Lutherans do not expect to be saved by obeying rules or being successful or upholding a correct theology, they do not need to be anxious about encountering unfamiliar ideas or about uncovering new and deeper understandings of Christian teachings and practices. Luther was quite clear that doubts and questions and struggle would accompany the life of faith. The effect of these experiences would be to deepen faith, not to undermine it.

Lutherans are heirs to a distinctive outlook known as a theology of the cross. Not only does this call them to servanthood rather than a life of triumph, as has already been emphasized, but it also calls them to recognize the limits of human knowing. Even in the self-disclosure of revelation, God remains hidden. Believers cannot know God fully and cannot see the world from God's perspective. Their limits both obscure and distort the truth. As we have heard Paul say, God's judgments are unsearchable and his ways inscrutable. This means that we need to make a careful distinction between God and our understanding of God, and between God's grace and our description of God's grace. It means we have to be cautious about our claims to know what God can and cannot do. If we had all the answers, dialogue would be unnecessary. But when our knowledge is limited, we have things to learn, and dialogue provides an opportunity to do just that.

> We need to make a careful distinction between God and our understanding of God and between God's grace and our description of God's grace.

Lutherans also are heirs to a lively sense of vocation—to a calling that focuses more on serving the neighbor and the community in and through all areas of life than on following rules. A lively sense of vocation does not permit us to draw a line and declare that anyone on the other side of this line is beyond our concern. And a lively sense of vocation does not allow us to ignore civil engagement or advancing the common good.

Lutherans also benefit from Luther's distinction between two kingdoms. The God-given role of governments and authorities is different from the God-given role of our faith community. We are called to be citizens who care about all the people in our communities and in our nation. At one and the same time we are called to find mutual support and encouragement among those who share our faith. (To this distinction we will return below.)

And, finally, Lutherans have the experience of being "insiders/outsiders" in American culture. As roughly 3 percent of the population, Lutherans do not perceive Christianity or the relationship between Christianity and society in the same way as do the dominant forms of Christianity. Given the idea of the two kingdoms, Lutherans do not expect the nation to legislate "godly laws." Nor do they think they know exactly what God is up to. They are not surprised by the complex mixture of good and evil evidenced by people everywhere, including in their religious practices. Nor do they think God has given up on the world and is preparing for its destruction. They do not distrust learning and science. As "insiders/outsiders" they can empathize with all the doubts a Muslim or a Jew or the member of any other religion might have about the rhetoric of a "Christian nation" or of an "exceptionalism" that regards this nation to be divinely appointed to instruct and to police the rest of the world.

All of the items that have been highlighted in this section are gifts to our age from the Lutheran tradition. In an ecumenical age, when the gifts of any Christian tradition are available to all, these are offered to all believers for their use as they sort out their relation to persons in other religions.

In Summary: Why Practice Inter-Religious Dialogue and Cooperation?

Let us conclude with a brief summary (already anticipated in the last section of the Introduction). Given all that we have been saying, there are several reasons to practice inter-religious dialogue and inter-religious cooperation.

One is our calling to serve the neighbor. Getting to know the neighbor is crucial if we are to serve that person or that person's community.

Closely related to this is a second. Members of other religions are often harmed when stereotypes are allowed to circulate without objection or correction. Finding out enough to challenge misinformation contributes to the well-being of our neighbors and the well-being of society as a whole.

Third, a growing number of Americans describe themselves as spiritual but not religious. Most of them believe in God or in a spiritual being but are disillusioned with the church. The reasons are many, but one of them is its historical exclusivism. They have trouble believing that their non-Christian friends are total outsiders in God's kingdom and under divine condemnation. Just as Martin Luther saw God's hand at work even in challenges to the church (such as that posed by the Turks who were threatening to overrun Germany), so God's hand may be at work in this challenge. In the voices of the church's critics, God may be calling Christians to move beyond the triumphalism of claiming exclusive rights to the truth to a more humble and open exploration patterned after the way of the cross. This does *not* mean saying that all religions are the same *nor* that they are all paths to the same goal. Nor does it mean abandoning or lessening our commitment to the faith. It does mean reserving judgment and exploring whether we have something to learn from those whose religious outlook differs from our own.

> In the voices of the church's critics, God may be calling Christians to move beyond the triumphalism of claiming exclusive rights to the truth to a more humble and open exploration patterned after the way of the cross."

Fourth, Christians are called to be peacemakers. With all of the forces in our world that fragment and divide peoples, inter-religious cooperation has the potential to bring them together.

A fifth reason is the benefit it can bring to the Christian, whose own understanding of faith is typically deepened and enhanced in the process.

And a sixth has to do with our calling to be good citizens. This reason may need some additional explanation. Christians in the United States live in a society that is "pluralistic." Not only are all the major religions of the world represented here, and not only are they all to be tolerated, but they also all have the same constitutional standing with regard to the government. "Pluralism" means that none has a privileged position and that Christians should not expect the government to pass laws that favor Christians, even though they have historically been in the majority. It is instead the responsibility of every citizen—Christian, Muslim, Jewish, Hindu, Buddhist—to distinguish between what is good for the population as a whole and what is good for their particular group. The only way citizens can do this is to build relations with members of other religions so that they can sort out together what actually serves the common good. Otherwise, how is one to know?

To take this one step further, there are contributions that religions, when they work together, can make to society as a whole. For example, they have a shared interest in religious freedom. They have a shared interest in human dignity. They have a shared interest in feeding the hungry, providing access to health care, and insuring economic opportunity for all. They have a shared interest in healthy families and healthy communities. Although sometimes it is forgotten as they fall victim to their own fear, they have a shared interest in fostering the wholeness of all humans and in all the conditions that make this possible. None of these shared goals can be attained in isolation or via religious conflict. Rather, the members of the various religions need to work together. And if they do work together, they can have a much more credible influence on public policy than if they remain isolated. So, this sixth reason for engaging in inter-religious dialogue and cooperation is to be able to maximize the benefits Christians and others can contribute to society as a whole. There is little doubt that our fractured world needs their contribution.

While recognizing that the road to inter-religious understanding can be a demanding pilgrimage with not all the theological questions settled in advance, the purpose of this book has been to provide encouragement (theological encouragement and practical encouragement) to engage in respectful conversation and cooperation.

Its next chapter is in your hands.

FOR DISCUSSION

1. Faced with stereotypes of other religions, to what does the eighth commandment call us? What sort of response is appropriate? Note Luther's explanation: "We are to fear and love God, so that we do not tell lies about our neighbors, betray or slander them, or destroy their reputations. Instead we are to come to their defense, speak well of them, and interpret everything they do in the best possible light" (translation by Timothy Wengert in The Book of Concord, Fortress Press, 2000).

2. The Conclusion emphasizes the importance of providing hospitality and receiving hospitality. What are the implications of this in your own community? What are its implications with regard to refugees and immigrants whose religion and culture may be unlike your own?

3. Do you agree that faith can and does live with unanswered questions? What difference does this make in the way a believer treats others? What are some examples from the past or from this book or from your own experience?

Appendices

WAYS TO USE THIS BOOK

Whether you are reading this book for individual enrichment or as the leader of a group study, we invite you to begin by reflecting on these words from the Foreword by Presiding Bishop Elizabeth A. Eaton:

> This book invites us all into conversation by challenging us to reflect on our past, learn from our present, and en-vision the future to which God is calling us. The heart of the book is the real-life case studies of inter-religious relations unfolding in a variety of ELCA ministry contexts. They encourage us to understand that our questions, doubts, and failures are as important as our answers, convictions, and successes. They challenge us to embrace that while there are a variety of responses to religious plurality, our common response is rooted in our Lutheran vocation – our response to God's love in Jesus Christ.

And on these from Darrell Jodock's concluding remarks:

> While recognizing that the road to inter-religious under-standing can be a demanding pilgrimage with not all the theological questions settled in advance, the purpose of this book has been to provide encouragement (theological encouragement and practical encouragement) to engage in respectful conversation and cooperation.

> Its next chapter is in your hands.

Settings for Study and Discussion

This study guide is intended to help you write that next chapter in a variety of settings, from congregation to community to educational institution. The case studies in this book demonstrate many settings in which inter-religious life is happening, and these same settings can be places and occasions for study and discussion of the book:

- Congregational adult forum
- Rostered leader events

- Youth retreat
- College or seminary course and/or campus ministry
- Lay schools
- Inter-religious study groups
- Community organization meetings, such as a Habitat for Humanity group
- Service providers in-service training, such as in hospitals and prisons

Sample Formats for Study and Discussion

- A weekly or monthly congregational study series looking at all the chapters in sequence
- An undergraduate or seminary course discussing one or more chapters in seminar or online forum
- A two-hour one-time large group event, preferably among participants from several religious traditions, to highlight key ideas in the book and initiate small group intensive study of one or more chapters
- A half-day retreat, using one or more chapters
- A full-day retreat, combining discussion of one or more chapters with a short video and/or an inter-religious panel discussion

The Leader's Role

The primary leadership responsibilities are to:

- Plan the overall study and individual sessions, perhaps as part of a committee;
- Create an atmosphere of welcome and hospitality;
- Facilitate the discussion, using questions from each chapter and encouraging members to participate and listen to one another;
- Monitor schedule and time, ensuring that the group has a chance for discussion of the elements of the study that are most important or interesting for the group; and
- Share specific information from the book, its appendices, and other resources helpful for the group.

Using "Living with the Questions" to Develop a Study Forum and/or Series

You may plan a series taking each chapter (including the introduction, "Time-Tested Questions") in order and using the discussion questions provided. Chapters Two and Four especially could each form the basis for several sessions. Each group of case studies can be discussed independently or along with the chapters.

Additionally, Darrell Jodock's concluding remarks, "Living with the Questions," can be used as the basis for

- a one-session forum on this book
- the introductory or concluding session for a series
- the outline for a series of six to ten forums using the entire book.

Here's a summary of its contents with links to related material in the other chapters, where you may find pertinent discussion questions. The topics listed below could be combined into a single forum of one to two hours, or expanded to provide material for a full series.

1. Introducing religious diversity (pages 167-168)

Christians in North America have experienced religious diversity since the 15th century; and inter-religious conflict dates back many centuries.

Introduction, page 11-17
Chapter One, pages 25-30
Chapter Two, pages 48-49
Chapter Three, pages 99-100
Chapter Four, pages 121-124

2. Ways Lutheran Christians can engage non-Christian neighbors (pages 169-170)

We Christians are called to practice mutual hospitality with every human being, including people of other religious traditions. (See question 2, page 177.)

Chapter One, pages 36-40
Case Studies 1: Mutual Hospitality, pages 45-47
Chapter Two, pages 53-55
Chapter Three, pages 101-102
Chapter Four, pages 156-158

3. Christian approaches to other religions (pages 170-172)

The Bible can guide our re-thinking of engagement with inter-religious neighbors.

4. Christian life as relational (pages 172-173)

"Christianity is a way of life" that puts us into "relationship with God, other humans, and with the rest of creation." Similarly, other major religions are also ways of life, and we can focus on ourselves as persons meeting other persons in their own life experiences. And as we develop authentic friendships, we can let our witness to the good news shine through.

5. Dealing with discomfort and difficult questions (pages 171-172)

Experiencing discomfort in inter-religious encounters is normal, and this book offers strategies for learning to "fear not" (page 170). The Bible and Martin Luther both reassure us that we need not expect direct and complete answers to every question. (See question 3, page 177.)

6. Being a Lutheran Christian in a multi-religious world (pages 173-175)

Lutheran Christians are equipped for inter-religious understanding and relationships through our experience of God's grace, our trust in God's promises, our call to servanthood, our sense of vocation, our understanding of our roles as people of God and as citizens of our civil societies, and our experience of being both insiders and outsiders in American culture.

7. **Reasons for practicing inter-religious dialogue and cooperation (pages 175-177)**

   - Our calling to serve the neighbor

   - Our responsibility to challenge harmful stereotypes (See Foreword, Chapter One pages 30-34, Chapter Two pages 70-73, and question 1 page 177.)

   - Our capacity to learn from the voices and lives of others

   - Our calling to be peacemakers

   - Deepening our own faith

   - Our calling to be good citizens in a pluralistic society and to contribute to the welfare of all

For downloadable resources to support the use of this book, please visit: www.elca.org/en/Faith/Ecumenical-and-Inter-Religious-Relations/Inter-Religious-Relations/Case-Studies

If you want to learn more about:

- **The history of ELCA inter-religious engagement**, go to the Introduction, "Time-Tested Questions," pages 12-17, and "New Realities, New Thinking Since 1990," pages 25-30.

- **Ways the ELCA has interacted with American Muslim and Jewish neighbors**, go to "Time-Tested Questions" pages 13-16.

- **How Martin Luther's theology of vocation relates to inter-religious engagement,** go to "Time-Tested Questions" pages 17-21.

- **Some reasons to engage inter-religious others,** go to "Time-Tested Questions," pages 22-24; Guidelines for Interacting in the Real World, page 56; and "Living with the Questions," pages 168-177.

- **Inter-religious life at ELCA colleges and seminaries,** go to "New Realities, New Thinking Since 1990," pages 27-28; "Guidelines for Interacting in the Real World," pages 61-62; and Case Studies 3, pages 112-120 and Case Studies 4, pages 159-167.

- **How the Bible can help guide our inter-religious relations,** go to Introduction, pages 17-18, 20-21; "New Realities, New Thinking Since 1990," pages 30-31 and 34-36; "Guidelines for Interacting in the Real World," page 64-66; "Exploring the Uncomfortable Questions: The Experience of Inter-Religious Work, pages 90-92; "Our God and Their God: A Relational Theology of Religious Plurality," pages 126-128, 141-143, 145-148; and "Living with the Questions," pages 170-171.

- **The practice of hospitality with religious others,** go to "New Realities, New Thinking Since 1990," pages 36-40; "Guidelines for Interacting in the Real World," pages 53-57; "Our God and Their God: A Relational Theology of Religious Plurality," pages 156-158, and Case Studies 1, pages 45-47.

- **Ways to become a pilgrim in a multi-religious context,** go to "New Realities, New Thinking Since 1990," pages 40-43.

- **Insights for planning multi-faith worship events,** go to "Guidelines for Interacting in the Real World," pages 50-53; and "Our God and Their God: A Relational Theology of Religious Plurality," pages 121-123.

- **Deepening theological conversation with others,** go to "Guidelines for Interacting in the Real World," pages 59-64; "New Realities, New Thinking Since 1990," pages 40-42; and Case Studies 3, pages 112-120.

- **How people from many religious groups are collaborating to address civil society concerns**, go to "Guidelines for Interacting in the Real World," pages 70-74; "Exploring The Uncomfortable Questions: The Experience of Inter-Religious Work, pages 88-89; and Case Studies 2, 82-87.

- **Religious diversity as it affects the U.S. military,** go to Guidelines for Interacting in the Real World," page 77; and Case Studies 2, 82-85.

- **Ways of understanding God in the context of inter-religious dialogue**, go to "Exploring the Uncomfortable Questions: The Experience of Inter-Religious Work, pages 93-98; and "Our God and Their God: A Relational Theology of Religious Plurality," pages 124-133.

- **How we profess Jesus Christ among the religions,** go to "Our God and Their God: A Relational Theology of Religious Plurality," pages 137-141 and 144-152.

- **Balancing inter-religious engagement with Christian mission and evangelism**, go to "Exploring the Uncomfortable Questions: The Experience of Inter-Religious Work, pages 93-94 and 99-104; and "Our God and Their God: A Relational Theology of Religious Plurality," pages 134-136 and 153-156.

- **The ethics of responding to neighbors of different faiths**, go to "Exploring the Uncomfortable Questions: The Experience of Inter-Religious Work," pages 104-109.

- **The role of prayer in our journey toward inter-religious understanding**, go to "Our God and Their God: A Relational Theology of Religious Plurality," pages 121-122 and 124-128.

- **What we can learn from Luther's dealings with religious others**, go to "Time-Tested Questions," pages 14-15; New Realities, New Thinking Since 1990, pages 31-33; "Our God and Their God: A Relational Theology of Religious Plurality," page 136.

- **New ways of thinking about salvation**, go to "Our God and Their God: A Relational Theology of Religious Plurality," pages 145-152.

- **Engaging others in a conflict-filled world**, go to "Exploring the Uncomfortable Questions: The Experience of Inter-Religious Work, pages 88-89; Case Studies 2, pages 82-87; and "Living with the Questions: Concluding Remarks," pages 173-175.

- **Some ways Lutherans are equipped for multi-religious life**, go to "Time-Tested Questions," pages 19-22, "New Realities, New Thinking Since 1990," pages 25-30; "Exploring the Uncomfortable Questions: The Experience of Inter-Religious Work, pages 94-98; "Our God and Their God: A Relational Theology of Religious Plurality," pages 145-148; and "Living with the Questions," pages 169-170 and 172-175.

NOTES ON CONTRIBUTORS

Authors and Editors

Jonathan Brockopp, Ph.D., is associate professor of history and religious studies at Pennsylvania State University and serves on the ELCA Consultative Panel on Lutheran-Muslim Relations. In addition to publications in early Islamic legal history, he is co-author (with Jacob Neusner and Tamara Sonn) of *Judaism and Islam in Practice: A Sourcebook* (Routledge, 2000), contributor to the Pilgrim Library of World Religions (1997-2000), editor of two volumes on Muslim ethical thought (2003 and 2008), and editor of the *Cambridge Companion to Muhammad* (2010).

Darrell Jodock (consulting editor), Ph.D., is the Drell and Adeline Bernhardson Distinguished Professor Emeritus at Gustavus Adolphus College in St. Peter, Minnesota, and a pastor in the ELCA. He chairs the ELCA Consultative Panel on Lutheran-Jewish Relations and represents the ELCA at the Convening Table on Inter-Religious Relations of the National Council of Churches. He is the editor and co-author of *Covenantal Conversations: Christians in Dialogue with Jews and Judaism* (2008).

Carol Schersten LaHurd (editor), Ph.D., serves as adjunct professor at the Lutheran School of Theology at Chicago and outreach consultant for A Center of Christian-Muslim Engagement for Peace and Justice. From 2006 to 2010 she was coordinator of the ELCA's Middle East peace-making campaign and serves on the ELCA Consultative Panel on Lutheran-Muslim Relations and the editorial board of *Dialog: A Journal of Theology.* She is the author of two annual Bible studies for the Women of the ELCA: *Luke's Vision: the People of God* (1998) and *Transforming Life and Faith* (2014).

Kathryn Mary Lohre (consulting editor) is the assistant to the presiding bishop and executive for Ecumenical and Inter-Religious Relations in the Office of the Presiding Bishop of the Evangelical Lutheran Church in America. From 2012 to 2013 she served a two-year term as president of the National Council of the Churches of Christ in the USA, the first Lutheran and youngest woman, and edited the book *For Such a Time as This: Young Adults on the Future of the Church* (Judson Press, 2013). From 2003 to 2011, she served as assistant director of the Pluralism Project at Harvard University, Diana Eck's premier research project on religious diversity in the United States.

Esther Menn, Ph.D., is Dean and Vice President for Academic Affairs and Ralph W. and Marilyn R. Klein Professor of Old Testament/Hebrew

Bible at the Lutheran School of Theology at Chicago. She is a member of the ELCA Consultative Panel on Lutheran-Jewish Relations and of the Christian Scholars Group on Jewish Christian Relations.

J. Paul Rajashekar, Ph.D., is Luther D. Reed Professor of Systematic Theology, Director of the Asian Theological Summer Institute at The Lutheran Theological Seminary at Philadelphia, and a pastor of the Evangelical Lutheran Church in America. Originally from the India Evangelical Lutheran Church, he has previously served as professor of theology at The United Theological College, Bangalore, India; The Gurukul Theological College, Madras (Chennai), India; as Executive Secretary for Church and People of Other Faiths at the Department of Theology of The Lutheran World Federation, Geneva, Switzerland (1984-1991); and as Dean of the Lutheran Theological Seminary at Philadelphia (2000-2012). He has also served the ELCA in various capacities, including as an elected member of the ELCA Church Council.

Peg Schultz-Akerson, is a pastor of the Southwest California Synod (ELCA) and a certified spiritual director. She has served congregations in Modesto, Santa Monica, Newbury Park, Pasadena, and Chico, California, and on boards of interfaith councils in each of these communities. She is a member of the ELCA Consultative Panel on Lutheran-Jewish Relations.

Mark N. Swanson, doctor in Arabic and Islamic Studies (PISAI, Rome), is the Harold S. Vogelaar Professor of Christian-Muslim Studies and Interfaith Relations at the Lutheran School of Theology at Chicago. He chairs the ELCA Consultative Panel on Lutheran-Muslim Relations. His publications include *The Coptic Papacy in Islamic Egypt, 641-1517,* (Cairo, 2010) and other studies of Christian Arabic literature, the medieval Egyptian church, and the history of Christian-Muslim relations.

These additional colleagues from the ELCA Consultative Panels on Lutheran-Jewish and Lutheran-Muslim Relations also contributed significant material and editorial advice:

Ward (Skip) Cornett, III, former director of continuing education at Trinity Lutheran Seminary and ELCA pastor

Peter E. Makari, Ph.D., Area Executive for Middle East/Europe, United Church of Christ

Peter A. Pettit, Ph.D., Associate Professor of Religion Studies and Director of the Institute for Jewish-Christian Understanding, Muhlenberg College

Nelly Van Doorn Harder, Ph.D., Professor of Islamic Studies, Wake Forest University

Primary Case Study Authors

Caleb Arndt is a Lutheran Thousand Oaks, California, native who will be graduating from California Lutheran University in 2016 with degrees in English and Music Production. He was a key contributor to the grassroots interfaith movement at CLU, which eventually became Interfaith Allies. Caleb served as the first Interfaith Allies intern. At the core of his work is a passion for social justice and cross-cultural education.

Jacqueline Bussie, Ph.D., is Director of the Forum on Faith and Life and Professor of Religion at Concordia College in Moorhead, Minnesota. Bussie teaches and publishes in the areas of theology, service-learning, problem of evil studies, Christian ethics, interfaith cooperation, and faith and public life. She is a theologian, author, and public servant of the ELCA. Her first book, *The Laughter of the Oppressed* (2007), was the winner of the national Trinity Prize. Her second book, *Outlaw Christian: Finding Authentic Faith by Breaking the "Rules,"* to be published in April 2016, is written for lay folks who want to talk more about grief, joy, hope, doubt, and lament.

Rebecca Cardone served as President of the Associated Students of California Lutheran University 2012-2013. She graduated from CLU in Political Science and Global Studies, with minors in Philosophy and Religion, and she holds a master's degree in Women's Studies with a focus on gender-based violence from the University of Oxford, Exeter College. At the time of publication, Rebecca works for Lloyd's Register Quality Assurance, a certification body for international standards and corporate responsibility.

Allen I. Juda is Rabbi Emeritus of Congregation Brith Sholom (Conservative), Bethlehem, Pennsylvania, where he served for thirty-nine years, retiring in 2014. He has served as chair of the Lehigh Valley Jewish Clergy group and given leadership to the chaplaincy program at St. Luke's Hospital and Health Network. He has chaired the planning team for the Day of Dialogue for nearly two decades.

Joseph Kempf is a student (class of 2016) at Augsburg College in Minneapolis, where he is studying chemistry with a minor in religion. He hopes to have a career studying honeybees and colony collapse disorder, with an emphasis on sustainable agriculture.

Scottie R. Lloyd served as an ELCA chaplain in the United States Army Chaplaincy for nearly forty years active and reserve. Ministering in Europe, Korea, the Middle East, Haiti, and across the United States, he retired in 2012, serving in his last position as the Director of Personnel and Ecclesiastical Relations for the Army Chief of Chaplains. A graduate of Christ Seminary-Seminex (1983), he currently serves as the pastor of The Lutheran Church of Our Savior in San Bernardino, California.

Richard W. Priggie is in his seventeeth year as Chaplain of Augustana College, Rock Island, Illinois, his alma mater. Prior to this position, Rev. Priggie served as pastor of ELCA congregations in Massachusetts, Connecticut, and Illinois. In addition to leading a multi-faceted interfaith understanding effort on campus, Rev. Priggie teaches a very popular elective course in the academic curriculum each year, titled *The Soul of Harry Potter.*

Sara Trumm is the Program Coordinator at A Center of Christian-Muslim Engagement for Peace and Justice, Lutheran School of Theology at Chicago. Previously she served at Holden Village, Youth Encounter, Global Mission Institute at Luther Seminary, and the Henry Martyn Institute in Hyderabad, India. She enjoys bridging cultures and faith traditions through music, service, and food.

HELPFUL WEBSITES FROM THE EVANGELICAL LUTHERAN CHURCH IN AMERICA AND PARTNER ORGANIZATIONS

ELCA Inter-Religious Resources

Downloadables, such as those listed below:

www.elca.org/Resources/Ecumenical-and-Inter-Religious-Relations

Covenantal Conversations: Christians in Dialogue with Jews & Judaism

The Declaration of the ELCA to the Jewish Community

Discover Islam Study Guides

Guidelines for Lutheran-Jewish Relations

Talking Points: Christian-Jewish; Christian-Muslim

Why Follow Luther Past 2017? A Contemporary Lutheran Approach to Inter-Religious Relations

Windows for Understanding

Quicklinks to many online resources:

www.elca.org/en/Faith/Ecumenical-and-Inter-Religious-Relations/Inter-Religious-Relations/Online-Resources

ELCA Academic Centers and Institutes

A Center of Christian-Muslim Engagement for Peace and Justice of the Lutheran School of Theology at Chicago
http://centers.lstc.edu/ccme/

Muhlenberg College Institute for Jewish-Christian Understanding
www.muhlenberg.edu/cultural/ijcu/

Ecumenical Partner Inter-Religious Websites

Episcopal Church USA
www.episcopalchurch.org/page/ecumenical-interreligious

Presbyterian Church USA
http://gamc.pcusa.org/ministries/interfaith/

United Church of Christ
www.ucc.org/ecumenical_interfaith-relations

United Methodist Church
www.gccuic-umc.org/

National Council of Churches Interreligious Relations
www.nationalcouncilofchurches.us/shared-ministry/interfaith/

Representative Multi-Religious Organizations

Council for a Parliament of the World's Religions: "…was created to cultivate harmony among the world's religious and spiritual communities… in order to achieve a just, peaceful and sustainable world." Since 1893 the Parliament has organized periodic conferences, inviting as speakers religious leaders from around the world.
www.parliamentofreligions.org/

The Guibord Center—Turning Religion Inside Out: "a non-profit organization that invites people to experience the transformative spirituality at the center of the world's great religions"
www.theguibordcenter.org

Interfaith Youth Core: works with American college students to produce "the interfaith leaders needed to make religion a bridge and not a barrier"
www.ifyc.org

The Pluralism Project at Harvard University: seeks to document "the contours of our multi-religious society, explore new forms of interfaith engagement, study the impact of religious diversity in civic life, and contextualize these findings within a global framework"
www.pluralism.org

Religions for Peace USA: "gathers representatives from the religious communities in the U.S.; promotes multi-religious cooperation for peace and justice; builds on the spiritual, human, and institutional resources of its communities; enhances mutual understanding; and acts for the common good"
www.rfpusa.org/

Shoulder to Shoulder Campaign: "an interfaith organization dedicated to ending anti-Muslim sentiment by strengthening the voice of freedom and peace"
www.shouldertoshouldercampaign.org/